Humble Journey:

More Precious Than Gold

Swin Cash

Empowering You Publishing LLC
1985 Lincoln Way, Suite 23-176
White Oak, PA 15131

Library of Congress Cataloging-in-Publication Data

Swin Cash,
Humble Journey: More Precious Than Gold
Edited by: Jakki Nance
Published by: Empowering You Publishing LLC, 1985 Lincoln Way, Suite 23-176, White Oak, PA 15131

Library of Congress Control Number: 2013934081
ISBN: 978-0-9889561-0-0

10 9 8 7 6 5 4 3 2 1

Printed in the United States of America

Note: The reader assumes all responsibility for the consequences of any actions taken based on the information presented in this book. The information in this book is based on the author's experience. Every attempt has been made to ensure that the information is accurate; however, the author cannot accept liability for any errors that may exist. The facts are subject to interpretation, and the conclusions and recommendations presented here may not agree with other interpretations.

This book is dedicated to all those who dream big.
Remember - winning the game is amazing...
but being in the game, and the journey to get there,
can be even more special.

Fourth Quarter...109

    Changing Seasons of My Life...........................109
    Another Call...112
    Almost There..114
    The Final Call...117
    Pre-Olympic Trip to London...........................122
    Starting Over...124
    Back to Seattle...125
    The Windy City..126
    The Olympic Games – The Finale.....................128

Note From The Author..137
Special Thanks...139

Contents

First Quarter 1

   The Beginning of the End.......................................1
   I Choose..2
   The Doctor's Call..4
   2008 Olympic Year 10
   The Trade 13
   The Call...19
   The Business of Basketball 25

Second Quarter 35

   Under the Knife..35
   The Recovery 42
   The Comeback Begins...45
   The China Experience...49
   The Storybook Season...55
   Off to Prague..64

Halftime 7

   Letting Go of Toxic Relationships.......................7
   How Love For CFK Helped Fill a Void...............8
   Positive People – Positive Influences ....

Third Quarter ....

   A New Focus..
   Building Blocks..
   Back To Business in the WNBA ....
   Olympic Hopes..

First Quarter

The Beginning of the End

I n the game of life sometimes things seem to get harder as we go. We may lose some quarters but our hope is that we will win the game. From one test to the next, each step was only preparation to be tested again; but as they say, the greater the test the greater the testimony. God has shown me over this journey that He is real and He never left my side. By the end of this book I hope you realize the same.

Before I can talk about how my journey started in 2008, I need to help you understand part of the origin of where it started. I tore my ACL in my left knee in 2004 after winning Olympic gold in Greece. ACL injuries are difficult to overcome; ask any athlete that's had one. An ACL injury ends up impacting your entire body and your game more than you realize. Once you recognize the impact, you can end up with another major pain – literally.

Even though I tore my ACL in 2004, years later I was still feeling the effects. I wasn't playing my best. Additionally, I had developed an issue in my back because of it. It was 2007. I was playing in Detroit for the Shock. At the time, all I remember was the pain. Who knew those injuries would end up saving my life?

I Choose

The Detroit Shock was coached by one of the original bad boys from the Detroit Pistons, Bill Laimbeer. He demanded a lot of his players and I went into the season not at 100 percent. It was frustrating for me because I always push myself, on and off the court. Add to that the mental test of trying to figure out what my role on the team was going to be and I was really having trouble.

You have to understand basketball team dynamics. Yes, I was still the Captain, but the dynamics of the team were changing. I wasn't the strongest player and everyone knew that. I wasn't playing my best. Plus, my close friend Ruth Riley was gone and she had always had my back on and off the court. Now there was just me and I felt isolated and alone. My body wasn't the same. My game wasn't the same. The team wasn't the same.

If you've ever been injured then you understand that it's not only that part of your body that's affected but your mind is as well. I was subconsciously catering to that injury and I forced the rest of my body to overcompensate for it. Basketball is as much a mental sport as it is physical and if your mind isn't in it then your body isn't much good. I wasn't my normal self and I know people watching me could tell it as well.

Despite being 70% healthy Bill still entrusted me enough to be the captain, which I had been since 2003. He didn't have multiple captains like some coaches do. Being the only captain was bittersweet though, like a gift and a curse. It's really hard to lead when you're a wounded captain. Imagine playing in a basketball game with a hundred pound jacket on your back and a myriad of thoughts running through your mind. That was my game at that point. My body was breaking down more every day. I was starting to wonder if I'd aged a couple more years and forgot to count them. There was a constant pain in my back that began to wear me down. It hurt to sit, to walk, and to run, basically to do anything. I'm not the type to make excuses nor do I love running to the doctor. I'm kind of old fashioned when it comes to my game. I play through pain and I have a very high tolerance for it. But this pain made me give in. I decided to go to the doctor to be checked out.

I went in for what I thought was a routine MRI. I figured they would find a bulging disc in my back or something like that. I waited for the results to come and a couple days later I received a call from the doctor.

The Doctor's Call

I still remember answering the phone and hearing the doctor's voice. It was so matter-of-fact. He told me when they looked at the MRI they saw something on my kidney. I needed to come in. He said it was a tumor and that they needed to see if it was cancerous.

Suddenly I couldn't hear anything. My entire world went completely silent. My chest was moving slowly but I couldn't hear my breath. I opened my mouth as if to speak, and truly thought I had, but nothing came out. I hadn't said a word. He asked if I was still there. I finally spoke up and I asked him if he could repeat himself. He told me again just as emo-tionlessly as he'd told me the first time. I realized that I wasn't dreaming and I'd heard him right. As quickly as my world had stopped, it began to race. My mind was a whirlwind of questions, thoughts and memo-ries; memories of my aunt, who had passed away from cancer, thoughts of the fact that cancer ran in my family, and questions about what was next for me. Would cancer claim me just as it had my aunt? She had fought a courageous battle but ultimately she did not get to finish out her game. Cancer took her out early. Would I have the same fate? Would I never make it to the fourth quarter?

I went back in and had a procedure to test the tumor. It came back that it was malignant. I did have cancer. The devil that had taken my aunt out of the game was now after me. The doctors said it would need to be removed, but they told me they didn't have to remove it right then. It could wait until after the season was over. What?!? Are you kidding me? You're telling me that I have cancer in my body and you want me to live with it inside of me while I play basketball? That was my understanding of it. The doctor let me know that it wasn't as bad as I was thinking. He assured me that it wouldn't spread and that I'd be ok because I'm young and it had been caught early.

I remember that he called me lucky. But I called it blessed. If I hadn't had the back pain, I wouldn't have gone to the doctor and the cancer might have continued to grow and spread. God was looking out for me and allowed me to catch it before it got worse.

I listened to the doctor and I went back to play. I was still in a lot of pain because I did in fact have a herniated disc but I wasn't going to have surgery for it. I figured I'd just do some strength and conditioning for the disc and have surgery for the tumor. I decided I didn't want anyone to know, other than my coach. I didn't want my teammates to know. I didn't want the media to know. I didn't want anyone to know other than the people that absolutely needed to know. I didn't want anyone to make any excuses for me. I didn't want to blame the way I was playing on the tumor in my body. I'm not the type of person that looks for an escape or an excuse. I'd rather run through my problems than to run around them. I continued to play. The pain didn't go away. In fact it was fighting me with a vengeance. Only Coach Laimbeer and the trainer knew what was going on in my body. They knew I was playing every playoff game, working out at every training session, attending every practice, while dealing with the physical and mental effects of a herniated disk and cancer.

We kept playing and we kept winning. It's amazing when I look back at the challenges within our team and think about the fact that we kept winning. We made it to the finals. Keep in mind that I had received the news about the tumor on my kidney only a couple weeks before the playoffs. I was trying to stay positive and trust that what the doctors told me was true. That can be one of the hardest things to do when you feel like your life is on the line. I couldn't get my head in the game though. I kept fighting and my team kept growing further apart. I remember there was a game in the playoffs, I believe it was game two of the eastern conference finals, and my coach benched me because he felt that I wasn't playing hard enough. I remember reading in the paper that he felt like I wasn't playing at my best and that I wasn't giving as much as I should. It was something to that effect. I remember how it made me feel. I was so hurt because I knew that he knew what I was going through. Looking back I know he was just doing his job and I don't think he meant to hurt me. It was just his explanation of the situation. My mind was analyzing everything.

I was given the opportunity to keep playing and we made it to the deciding game five of the WNBA finals. We were playing the Phoenix Mercury. Game five was on our home court so it was an electrifying atmosphere. There were 20,000 fans in the building and this was huge. Unfortunately, we came into the game with so much on our minds and so much baggage under our bench that it hurt us that night. We played horribly and they blew us out by 19 points. The final buzzer sounded and a silence came over the crowd. The Mercury were jumping, laughing, and celebrating all over our court. I remember looking into the crowd and waving at our fans. It was a farewell wave. I knew instinctively that it was the last dance for me in a Detroit Shock jersey. Detroit had been good to me but it was time for me to go my own way.

It had been rumored that there were trade talks for me but most people didn't know that I was the one that requested the trade, not the team. I knew that night would be my last night in that jersey. After the game, I sat in the locker room exhausted, like a wounded soldier after a long war. A photographer snapped a picture of me in this moment and it was in the paper the next day. Looking at that picture, I knew what they meant when they said a picture is worth a thousand words. That picture said a lot. You could see the pain of defeat. The anguish of my emotions was right there. The caption read: Will this be the last time we see Swin in a Shock jersey? I remember answering aloud to myself, "yep!" I knew I was done there. There was too much going on and I needed a fresh start. Not only had we lost a deciding game, but we had allowed it to happen on our court. As a fierce competitor, that was a hard one to take. Add to that, our locker room had become a negative environment instead of a place of peace and unity. There was an organizational disconnect for me and I needed a break. I did not need added drama in my life right now.

I realized that my health would not improve if my professional life did not change. A new team and a new environment would be good for me, mentally and physically. Trust me, after you've been told you have cancer, you are always willing to make serious changes in your life to make sure you have a life to live.

Two days after my final game as a Detroit Shock I went to have my surgery to remove the tumor on my kidney. I was still terrified. I could only hope that everything would go as planned. The surgery and result was out of my hands. I had to trust in the hands of my surgeons and the staff. And ultimately, I had to put it all in God's hands. I had to let go. He would handle this one.

After the cancer surgery, I began to do the necessary things to prepare for the Olympic trials that would be coming up. (You have to understand the mindset of an athlete. Not even cancer stops us for too long...) I knew I didn't have the best season that year and now there were trade rumors swirling around me. So much was up in the air. I felt like the aura around my name wasn't a good one following that season. People say that being traded doesn't matter, but I felt differently. A trade usually symbolizes something negative. A trade is rarely seen as a smart business move. It's usually seen as a player that is having issues either on or off the court or can't get along with the staff and teammates. That's not the way you want someone looking at you when you're trying to make an Olympic team.

I knew I had to put myself in the best light that I could, considering the situation I was in. I decided to go the extra mile. They say that there's no traffic on the extra mile and I was hoping that would be the case. I remember the US Olympic committee saying that there would be some trial sessions and that the more that we could come to them, the better it would make our chances of making the team. I decided to forego some overseas opportunities and sacrifice the money to stay in the US, so I wouldn't miss a session. It was my dream to make it on the 2008 Olympic team because I felt like that would be my year. I would be on the team with my girls Diana, Sue and Catch and I wanted that more than anything else at that time. As they say, "Anything worth having is worth sacrificing for." I took that saying to heart, so I sacrificed time, money and health, and I made the sessions. It didn't matter to me who else was there or who else wasn't. All that mattered was that I was doing what I could. I knew that I couldn't miss a session, so I didn't.

2008 Olympic Year

I started off 2008 very focused. This was it. This was the year of the Olympic games. I knew I needed to be zoned in so that I could put my best foot forward. As a pleasant surprise, the NBA called me to participate in the NBA All-Star Weekend festivities. They asked me to be a part of the Shooting Stars competition. The team consisted of an NBA legend, a rising star, and a WNBA player from the same city. My team had my coach from the Detroit Shock, Bill Laimbeer, and Chauncey Billups from the Pistons. Many people were asking me if it was going to be awkward to be on the same team with Bill because the media had speculated that I hated Bill and that's why I wanted to be traded. There were a lot of rumors swirling around about our relationship. People assumed that this meet up would be very awkward for both of us.

Bill and I had a sit down before we played in the competition. We spoke about my time in Detroit and the talk about me wanting to be traded. He asked me if I really wanted this or if it was more my agents pushing me? I confirmed my desire to be traded with him and let him know it was my decision to move on. Honestly, at the time I wanted to say more. I wanted to say that I was disappointed by some of his actions. I wanted to say I was hurt he benched me when he knew I was dealing with this health scare. But I didn't. I wasn't ready. I needed to let those wounds heal.

So I told him there was no ill-will, but it was just time for me to move on. In business as in life, you have to know when your time has come to change directions. You have to know when you need a fresh start. Have you ever had a favorite pair of shoes but after you wore them too much you realized you had to give in and get a new pair? Maybe you wore a hole in the sole or just wore them out so they didn't fit anymore? You don't love those shoes any less, you just know they don't fit you quite the same and it's time for a new pair.

Bill understood the x's and o's of winning. And I had been blessed to be part of a team that had won two WNBA Championships in Detroit. But I wasn't winning in this game called life and for me that was more important than any basketball dynasty. Detroit had given me a lot, and for that I will always be grateful. But now it was time to take my life back, my career back and start this new journey. Yes, our team was a Championship contender and I could have won another ring had I stayed, but that didn't matter to me as much as my happiness did. I'd rather have peace of mind and happiness more than another ring. It was time for me to go. (I always teach my niece a lady keeps it classy and that's exactly what I planned to do!) Coach Bill and I ended on a good note and he understood fully where I was coming from. We shook hands and I told him, "Let's go out here and win one more for Detroit!" That night we did just that. We played in the Shooting Stars competition and we won! I remember being on the stage accepting the award with this big old smile on my face. I was enjoying the moment. Hey, winning is always fun! So after they finished up our interview I grabbed the mic and I did our Detroit chant one last time! "Deeeeeeetroit Basketball." I was a great moment as Chauncey and Bill joined in the chant. I was at peace, I knew I was getting ready to leave the great city of Detroit but I knew I'd been a part of a great era there.

The Trade

The Monday right after the NBA All-Star weekend I received a call that I was traded to the Seattle Storm. It was a bittersweet feeling at the moment. It's like knowing you failed an exam but still seeing the result completely sucks. Through discussions with my agent Mike Cound, I knew the Shock wouldn't trade me to an Eastern Conference team. That was typical. I also knew Seattle was aggressively pursuing me. It was still a shock even though I knew it was coming; no pun intended. Anyways, I gathered myself and embraced the journey. Knowing in my heart the decision was right, but questioning in my psyche if this would hurt me from making the 2008 Olympic team. There were some pros and cons about this decision, but aren't there always? I mean each and every one of us make decisions about our careers, families, love life you name it. And with those deci-sions we must stand tall for whatever comes of them. The pros were that I would be on a veteran team with some great players. Sue Bird was my roommate in college, Tanisha Wright grew up in the town right next to me and from what could I see Lauren Jackson was one of the best players in the world.

Sue and I have always had this weird relationship. We were like sisters, sisters who fight a lot. Sometimes people would think we hated each other because we would argue and get mad at each other but once we were on the court our chemistry was amazing. Hey, what can I say, you put two ultra-competitive people together, one of whom always has to be right, (yeah that's Sue) and one of whom has to get the last word because she knows you want to be right, (that's me) and you get 6 championships together and over 15 years of friendship. I was excited about being on the same team with Sue. We had chemistry on the floor that no one could deny. We got drafted 1 and 2 in the WNBA draft and could have never imagined we would be playing together again. It was like a reunion for me in that aspect. Then there were other greats like Sheryl Swoopes and Yolanda Griffith that I heard were rumored to be coming to Seattle and I thought it was all a dream. I was beginning to think that this could be something great.

There was a downside to the trade though. I come from a very large family and we're all really close. It was always great being on the East Coast because I'm very close to my mother and family. Since high school they would make a lot of my games. Now to think I would be starting this new journey so far away was scary for a self-proclaimed momma's girl like me. Yes I'm a momma's girl and I'm proud of it. I saw friends that didn't have that parental support so I'm blessed I had that from my mom always. It was no problem for mom to jump on the road from Pittsburgh and come to Detroit to see a game. Things were about to change now. If my family wanted to come to a game it would be a 6-hour plane ride and much more expensive than a 4 hour drive. I didn't like the idea of not having my support system there with me in Seattle but I know that sometimes we have to take the bad with the good. I mean think about it, taking on a new challenge in this crazy world and not having the ones you love there to lean on. But that's when you have to have faith and courage to press on.

I flew into Seattle to start getting ready for the season that was approaching. There was a buzz going around about the potential of our team but deep down I knew that I might not be as effective as I'd hoped to be. I was still in a lot of pain from the herniated disc in my back and it limited my play. Although I was in a lot of pain, taking pills and injections just strong enough to maintain, I fought through it. I didn't want to get surgery on my back because I didn't want to ruin my shot at making the 2008 Olympic team. (So you are probably thinking this girl is crazy! Heck, I think I was saying it subconsciously too!)

So as I fought through the pain, I would go back and forth to Michigan to get check-ups every three months. Then a little thing called "Stress" kicked in. The problem with stress is it always impacts you more than you realize. It affects you mentally but it also affects you physically. I started losing weight, lots of it. Now I know as a woman that seems like a good thing but as an athlete who needs the muscle mass, losing weight when you aren't trying to is not good. That's when more injuries happen.

So there I was, trapped in a vicious cycle of poor choices that just wouldn't end. Pain led to stress. Stress led to weight loss. And weight loss just caused more pain, mentally and physically.

But I tried to get beyond it. It was the early part of 2008, and it was all about getting to Beijing for me. There were a couple US trials that we were supposed to attend so I sucked it up and I made it to them. I was still trying to show face and put myself in a good position to make the team. That was my whole focus. I just tried to block out the pain as best as I could.

The doctors told me that if I got shots in my back that it would help with the pain. But they also said my problem would still exist. OK. I figured if they could just help curb the pain then I'd be fine to play. What I didn't really understand at the time was that cortisone injections can make the injury worse but you can't feel it because the injection masks the pain. My back was almost numb. But when the pain would come back, it came back with a vengeance! It's like the dirty little secret of professional sports. Sometimes they can be helpful but in my case it was a short term fix with long term implications. When the shot wore off you're worse off than you were before you got it. During the summer of 2008, I received four shots in my back trying to fight through the pain. In my mind, I just couldn't get surgery yet and I had to trust in my strength in order to get through this time period.

It's hard to explain the pain that I was feeling in my back. Sharp movements would feel like someone was stabbing me with a steak knife in my lower spine. Sometimes it would feel like there were a thousand needles jumping up and down and then running down my legs occasionally. It would feel like there were lightning bolts being shot across my lower back. During different practices I would just lay on the floor in pain until the coach subbed me in. I was basically doing what I could to maintain. I couldn't see any further than making it through each day. I remember one of my doctors telling me I must have high pain tolerance because he had NO idea how I was playing through this injury. Looking back, frankly, neither do I.

On the flights to games, I would stand up in the back of the plane sometimes for the entire flight because it hurt so bad to sit for long periods of time. I can't tell you how grateful I am that the flight crews were so accommodating. I guess the pain must have been obvious, now that I look back.

Every athlete who trains for the Olympic team goes through a lot; many even suffer through injuries. But when you want something with all your heart and soul, you will literally do whatever it takes to achieve it, including almost sacrificing your own health and future. Haven't you ever wanted something so bad that you are willing to do whatever it takes?

I realize now that chasing the Olympic dream was an ultimate goal, but it was also a path of avoidance. As long as I was chasing that dream, I didn't have to face what was going on with my body, my life and my career. I was on a journey, but was I on the right path to complete that journey?

Have you ever had a dream but felt that you were sacrificing something of yourself in pursuing it. Then you and I have both been there. But what path do we take to remain true to ourselves? Every decision has an impact. And some decisions are not our own to make. But once made, we can choose our own way. So, where do we go from here?

The Call

One day before practice I was sitting in the locker room just about to head to the court and my phone rang. It was odd. I always try and get in "work-mode" before practice so I usually don't have my ringer on. I remember looking at it and wondering who would be calling now.

It was Carol Callan, the Women's National Team Director for USA Basketball. This was a call I needed to answer. I picked up the phone and greeted her as I always do. "Hi Carol." She said, "Hey Swin, you got a minute?" But she didn't sound like she usually did. I could tell something was different. "Yes."

The call may have only lasted a minute but it seemed like a lifetime. "I'm calling to inform you that the committee has made their decisions about the US Olympic team and unfortunately you weren't chosen as one of the 12 players."

I felt like I had swallowed a bomb that exploded. I couldn't speak at first. Then finally, I asked, "Was I chosen as an alternate?" (An alternate is a player that is named to the team just in case any injuries occur to any of the 12 players, then an alternate can replace them). "I'm sorry Swin but you weren't chosen as an alternate either." In a way, as she said it, I felt bad for her. I could hear it in her voice that she didn't want to make this call but it had to be made. So now comes reality! I knew I had done everything that they asked and I was at every trial but this wasn't the call I was waiting for. I'd endured all of the pain for a reason. My every hope was set on this moment. This was my only goal in 2008. It felt like I got shot, then died, then came back to life. Picture a fully inflated basketball, then picture it being stabbed with a knife and exploding. That's about how I felt. My every hope for that year was crushed. All of the pain that I endured felt like it was for nothing. I was crushed in every sense of the word. The tears began to well up in my eyes. I felt like I needed a gurney to come in and roll me out. My heart was sitting on the floor under a thousand pound weight and I couldn't breathe very well. All of the pain, all of the agony, all of the defeat, all of the sacrifice and then this is the news I got?

I couldn't think. I sat there for a few minutes in shock and then I got up to go to the sink to wash my face and try to look alive for practice. I remember Tanisha Wright coming in there and telling me that it was time to go out. She looked at me and could see that something was wrong. She asked if everything was ok with me. I told her yes but obviously she could tell I was lying. She urged me out to practice and I walked out there like a zombie. I was completely numb! My body was there but my mind was miles away.

I was in practice going through the motions. I was looking at the coach while he was talking but my mind wasn't in the gym that day. He was looking at me crazy and I was looking back at him even crazier. I just wasn't up for anything during that practice. I was moving slowly. It was like it wasn't my body. I was there but I wasn't. I remember doing a three man weave drill, making passes and crying as I was doing it. Who plays basketball with tears streaming down their face? I was doing just that. Sheryl Swoopes came up to me and asked me what was going on with me and I was trying not to answer her. Then Sue Bird came and asked me was everything ok and I tried to brush her off as well. I finally gave in and just burst. I told them that I got "the call" letting me know I hadn't made the Olympic team. Sue went up and told the coach what was going on but it didn't matter much. I kept practicing and somehow I made it through that practice. I don't know how I finished it but I did.

For the next few days, I just laid in my apartment in Seattle and cried on the couch. I would cry all day. I cried like someone near and dear to me passed away. I cried until I was empty but yet tears kept coming. A million thoughts ran through my mind but I was alone. I had no one there to comfort me, to hold me, to console me and let me know that everything would be ok. I was by myself dealing with the worst news I'd gotten in my playing career up until this point. I was thinking about the hopes and dreams I had to make the team and why I wanted it so badly. As I reflect back, that moment of reflection was bigger than not making the team. I was pouring out my tears for so much more. Later I would finally understand just why!

In 2004, I went to the Olympics with my former UCONN teammates but we were the babies on the team and it wasn't our show. This time around we were supposed to go over together. We would be veterans. We would be able to make our mark on this team. I was looking forward to being on the team with Sue Bird, Diana Taurasi, and Tamika Catchings. But it wasn't going to happen for me. I was so angry about it. I was so hurt. I did all I could and I'd lost out. I was praying and living my life the right way the whole time. I suffered through pain. I didn't miss any of the trials. It felt so unfair to me. Have you ever felt cheated, or frustrated by something you can't control? Why is that? The mind is like a land mine if you let it be.

I began questioning God. I asked God how could other people make it who didn't even know or acknowledge him but me his daughter be left out. I counted all my good deeds and all my prayers and wondered how this could happen to me after all the good I'd done and all the prayers I'd prayed. Isn't that always the first thing humans do, blame God? I mean it doesn't matter if you're religious or have little faith, when stuff hits the fan we blame God and want answers.

Well God answered me in spirit. He whispered into my spirit and let me know that life will test us sometimes but it's only preparation for something bigger. A setback is a setup for a come up, that's a statement I used to say when I was younger. He let me know that everything happens for a reason and that my future would be greater than my past. He let me know that just because my hopes were deferred, they were not denied. I came to realize that everything is timing and everything happens in seasons.

So what season of life are you in? One where you need to walk on, to grow or just to be still? You have to spend time with yourself. Whether you are a spiritual person or not, you must take some time to listen to your soul. To be still, focus on what's in front of you, beside you and most of all what you need to leave behind you. It wasn't my season or my time.

I found solace in growing to understand that I must have order in my life before I could have increase in my life. There were some things that I had to do in order to get ready for my next opportunity. God could have been sparing me even more pain and hurt. I could have gone over to the Olympic Games and made a fool of myself on the court with all the pain that I was in. God had a plan that I knew not of its complexities. His ways are not our ways and His thoughts are not our thoughts; they are higher than ours. This situation showed me that God truly does work in mysterious ways! We won't always understand them, but He will give us the strength to cope with whatever life hands us.

Nonetheless, it was a very tough and trying time. It was like walking on eggshells around my teammates because Sue and Lauren were going to the Olympics and I wasn't. They were going to get their chance but I'd missed mine. I didn't want to spoil their experience and they didn't want to be inconsiderate of my feelings, knowing the pain that I was experiencing from not being able to go. It was a tough balancing act and we were trying to be considerate of each other, especially Sue and I. I feel so bad for being on edge and Sue not being able to fully express the joy she must have felt about being selected a second time in a row. I also respect her for respecting my feelings and not making it worse. It was really tough but we found a way through it.

Finally it was time for me to let the hurt go and start trying to move on from this setback. It's easy to stay down when you fall, but the real test is how you get back up. People rarely remember the fall... most just remember the climb.

The Business of Basketball

After I began to move on from the pain of not making the Olympic team I started to look for my next move. It was almost August of 2008. During Olympic years, the WNBA gives the players 10 days off during the Olympics. Then we are just "in market," which means that we would practice and be available for signings or any events in the city. It's like time off, but not exactly.

As the Olympic break was approaching, I received a call from my agent notifying me that I'd been offered a spot as an analyst with NBC. I'd get to be in New York for two weeks and do halftime shows and some commentating during the women's Olympic basketball games. This was a great offer and it was a blessing considering that broadcasting is the field I want to work in after basketball. It couldn't have come at a better time in my eyes because I was so hurt from not being able to be on the team that this was the next best thing. It also made sense to me since the team doctors had declared me "inactive" for the entire month of August. So I was not going to be able to practice or do anything physical other than rehab.

In my mind, I was being offered a situation that was the next best thing to playing in the Olympics for a baller who was benched because of injury – I was going to cover the games! While the ladies would be at the Olympics putting in their work, I'd get a chance to work on building additional skills off the court. Unfortunately, nothing ever goes as smoothly as we think it will go.

My coach let my agent know that he wouldn't be ok with me going to NY for the two weeks of Olympic break to be an Olympic commentator, in spite of the fact that I had a doctor's diagnosis verifying that I was unable to practice and that we had 10 days off during the Olympics. Ultimately, the decision was left up to me, but I was told there would be repercussions if I chose to go to NY.

My life is a journey. And the decisions I make ultimately take me down the paths that I choose. So I prayed on it and I thought long and hard about it. I realized that I'm a brand and that means I'm the CEO of me. I needed to make the best decision for my career because no one else would have to live with the consequences of my choices but me. This was a great opportunity in my eyes and could really give me the chance to network with great people and make some good connections that could come in handy after basketball is over. Before making a decision, I spoke to my family, got feedback from my teammates and consulted with my doctors. With all of that input, I felt I could make an informed decision that would be the right decision for me and my future. So I chose to go to NY and accepted that I would have to deal with whatever consequences came my way as a result. But at least I knew I was in control of my life and my choices.

I wanted to seize the opportunity because who knows if another would come in the near future. We have freedom of choice but not freedom of conse-quence. I knew that there would be some repercus-sions for my decision but I was ready and willing to face them. I hopped on the plane and flew to the city of dreams to have a date with another part of my destiny. I felt at peace about my decision and that's what mattered the most to me. I'm sure NBC wouldn't have asked if they thought it would have gotten me in trouble. Regardless of the ins and outs, the who's, what's, and why's, I went.

I had a great time in NYC and I met a lot of incredi-ble people. It was very much worth it and I wouldn't change it for anything. While I was there I was fortu-nate enough to bump into the renowned Teresa Ed-wards. Teresa is one of the greatest women to ever play the game. She has 5 Olympic medals and a host of other accolades. It was amazing to be able to sit and talk with her. She happened to also be on the US Olympic Committee. We had a great conversation. I picked her brain and tried to make sense out of this summer. Hearing myself talk it out with Tee was just the form of therapy that I needed. She not only gave me advice and encouragement but also said she would workout with me while we both were there. I'm sure she could sense my confusion and frustration so she spoke into my life and I received every word of it.

I had a revelation that night. I realized that I wouldn't be a victim any longer and I had to look within myself and make things happen. No longer would I be angry and bitter. I would choose happiness, a future and health above the game itself. I had to release those negative and draining emotions. I vowed that I would turn on the switch and that I would make a comeback and earn a spot on the 2012 team. I decided that day and in that moment that my 2012 opportunity wouldn't be like my 2008 opportunity. I told myself that if I take care of Swin then everything else would fall into place. That I would be able to be proud of my decisions no matter what the outcome.

It was time that I accepted full responsibility and made some changes. Changes to prioritize the things in my life that truly mattered. It's easy to quit when you are disappointed or feel you got the short end of the stick. It takes a lot of resolve and courage to say, let me learn from my past to better my future.

After calling the Olympics in NYC I flew back to Seattle and started getting ready for the second half of our season. My coach benched me my first game back and hit me with a fine. Those were the consequences for my choice and I accepted them without complaining about it. I was a new person, with a new mindset. I was ready to start changing my life and moving towards my goals. I'd decided that I was going to turn it around, buckle down, and get back on track!

We finished the regular season as the #2 seed in the western conference. The stage was set for a match-up with the Storm's biggest rival, the L.A. Sparks. Since it was my first season with the Storm, I was aware of the rivalry between these two west coast teams but I quickly learned just how intense that rivalry truly was.

We knew it would be an uphill battle going into the playoffs after losing our leading scorer Lauren Jackson, one of the best in the world, to injury for the entire post season. I can't lie, I was so limited physically that it took every ounce of strength in my body to lace my shoes up and play that series. I knew I had to give it all I could no matter how much it hurt. It was like a mental tug of war between my mind and my body. One wanted rest, the other wanted to just win baby (as the late Al Davis would say).

The first game was in LA and we stumbled out of the gate early. Winning on the road in the playoffs is tough but even tougher when you spot your opponent a 10 point lead at the end of the first quarter. I would only play 10 minutes that game and despite a 17 point halftime deficit, we battled back only to lose by 8. We may have had injuries but we definitely had heart!

It was time to regroup and head back to Seattle to try and extend the series. In the playoffs, especially when faced with an elimination game, the best thing to do is take it one game at a time. Win today to play tomorrow! This time we were the aggressor to start the game jumping out to a 26-15 halftime lead. It was a defensive battle for both teams and by the end of the 3rd quarter we were up 21 points. I managed to play 13 minutes in that game, but I was still limited by injuries. I was happy we got the win and had a chance to finish LA off at home. I just hoped my body had something left in the tank for the final game of the series. I ended up playing a series high 20 minutes in that deciding game but I knew I wasn't able to do what I could normally do on the court. We were never able to find a rhythm offensively or slow them down defensively like in the previous game and failed to advance in the playoffs. I was disappointed I couldn't help my teammates and I was disappointed to have been eliminated on our home court. I vowed that next time we play the playoffs I would be healthy and able to play at the high level I was accustomed to so I could really be there for my team.

I needed a break after this season. It had been a rough year for me and I needed some rest! So I flew to the Bahamas with my boyfriend. I needed to kick back, clear my mind, and just relax. One night we were in the room and he turned on the TV. The final game in the WNBA finals was on. My old team, the Detroit Shock was playing in that game. I looked at him with the side eye and said: "Really? Are you really going to watch this game right now?" He said: "Yeah, why not? I like some of the players and it's your old team." I kind of felt like he was kicking me while I was down but I sucked it up because I know men aren't too emotional and sometimes can't pick up on the subtle signals we as women are trying to send. Eventually the game was over and Detroit had won. They were celebrating and jumping around, the confetti was falling, and everyone was happy. You know what? I was happy too. I was happy for them and for the City of Detroit. I wasn't upset that I'd left or that they'd won it without me. Everyone that knows me knows that I love to win. I'm a winner and I'm used to winning. It's in my DNA and I've always been on winning teams. I want nothing more than championships. For me to have peace and calm like I did and still be happy about the decision I had made really solidified in my heart that I'd made the right decision. I was happy for Detroit. But more importantly, I was happy that I had chosen the right path for my new journey. We turned the TV off and I went to sleep with a smile that night. Winning is one thing, but enjoying it while you do is even bigger.

I learned that night that we have to be comfortable with our decisions in this life. We only get one life to live and we have to live it in a way that's satisfying and leaves room for growth. Sometimes you have to put yourself first in order to be happy. No one will have to live with your regrets but you, so make sure that you don't have any. I made some tough decisions in my life and I lived with the repercussions of them. Most of them I'd never change and I'm proud that I made them. It feels good to not have regrets and to move on in life and not harbor hate, bitterness, and strife. I urge you to make the tough decisions with your best interest at heart. If you have to leave a situation then leave it and don't look back. Don't make yourself feel guilty for doing the right thing. You should never regret looking out for your own best interest because if you don't love yourself enough to do it then who will?

I could've been jealous of the Shock's win. I could've lived with regrets but how would that have helped me? It would have hindered me instead. Think about what you know you need to do and don't be afraid to do it. Count the cost and the consequences before you do it and be sure you're making the right move. Once it's done you can't take it back. It's better for you to measure ten times and cut once than to measure once and have to cut ten times.

I learned a lot in what I'd call the first quarter of one of the toughest games of my life. I had a lot of setbacks, a lot of heartaches, and a lot of headaches. It all made me a stronger person. I lived and I learned. First came the test and then came the lessons. Although it seems backwards, those lessons are actually preparing you for the next test. Everything I went through in the course of those 12 months felt like a lifetime but I decided to leave it there and keep moving forward. I accepted responsibility for my life. I started to get things in order so that my life could go higher. I forgave those that hurt me. I loved those that despised me. And I got better every day. This is life and life is about growth. If you're not growing mentally, emotionally, and spiritually then you're dying subconsciously.

Swin Cash

Second Quarter

Under the Knife

I was resting my back after the season and still thinking about getting surgery. But before I could make a decision I received a call from my agent that a team in Prague, Czech Republic wanted me to come over and play for them. Again, it was bittersweet news. I was excited about the incredible opportunity but I knew I still wasn't at 100% physically.

At this point I need to explain something to you that a lot of people don't realize. Playing in the WNBA is definitely a dream come true for female athletes around the world. But people assume WNBA players make salaries similar to NBA players. To be candid, the salary of an NBA rookie player drafted between 25-30 could cover the entire salary cap for one WNBA team! Don't get me wrong. We are doing what we love. However in order to make a living and support ourselves and our families, we usually have to take a second job playing overseas during the WNBA off-season. I share this with you because I had not taken that second job the year before because I wanted to attend all the Olympic trials. My bank account and bills suffered!

So now, when I needed to rest my back or prepare for surgery, I had a chance to take a second job so I could pay my bills and help "my family," which for me is my charity and my children in "Cash for Kids." We all know what it's like to have the security of some money in the bank. And a second job playing in Prague would give me that security when I needed it most.

I decided to go over and accept the offer. I was on so much medication and trying to do everything that I could to ease the pain in my back but nothing was working. The needle sensations, the sharp pains and feelings of fire in my spine, it was all there and multiplied by 10 at this point. It hurt to walk most days, so you can imagine what it was like trying to play. But I had to fight through it. I did it once before for the benefit of others so why not do it now for the benefit of my security and my future? So I packed my things and headed on my next journey to Praha, as Prague is known in the Czech Republic.

It was a beautiful place, with great tradition and a wonderful organization. The team I played for were the USK Praha. For three months I gave it my all. I tried to fight through it but eventually the pain won out. It was time. My basketball agents Mike Cound and Tom Cross did a conference call with me and my team. They talked about it and the team agreed to cut the contract and let me return to the states. They were very gracious and understanding and I really appreciated that. I will always appreciate their generosity and serious concern for my health. Their doctors weren't only worried about basketball. They voiced concerns about the stress and long term affects I could have on my body.

So in January I headed back home and made my first firm decision to have back surgery. I decided that I'd pushed my body to the limit and I needed to do something about it. Up until this point, I was behaving like Super Man (or should I say Woman) trying to save the planet. But I'd finally met my kryptonite called back injury and I needed some help. A piece of my disc had broken off and was pressing against my sciatic nerve. Trust me when I say that's nothing to play around with. This injury had now affected my whole life not only just basketball. Driving my car, sitting in a chair, picking up my niece, going to a movie theatre and even trying to sit through a movie. It had consumed my life and it was time.

I flew back to the states and started the process of getting surgery. I remembered the year before while playing with Seattle they sent me to a doctor in LA when we were in town to play against the LA Sparks. This doctor was said to be one of the best in the country. The team paid for me to go visit him and they had all my paper work sent down to him while we were in LA in 2008. Naturally I thought this would be the doctor I'd have performing my surgery. I really liked him the first time we'd met and he confirmed then that I needed surgery.

So for me it was basic routine - come home - head to LA - get surgery – then get my butt kicked in rehab! We called the doctor's office and had the appointment set up for me to come in and get the surgery done. I was ready to go under the knife so that I could get back to being healthy and back on my journey towards another Olympic Gold Medal. I wasn't done in the prime of my career. I would be back not because I wanted to, but because I had to. No one ever says "I want to be a role model," but once you have that platform you have no choice but to walk the runway in those shoes. I'm a fighter, always have been, always will be. I understand with "great visibility comes responsibility" so I had my boxing clothes on ready to rumble through this battle. Trust me. I knew going through back surgery and rehab would be a battle. What I didn't know was that I had to fight another battle first.

It always seems to come down to a phone call with me. This was another bad one. Here I was, mentally prepared for back surgery, comfortable with the doctor I had chosen, and I get another call.

It was my team trainer in Seattle telling me that I couldn't have the surgery done by the doctor in LA. I heard the sadness in my trainer's voice. He didn't want to tell me I couldn't do it there. But the insurance wouldn't cover the surgery if I did it with him. It didn't matter that my body and my physical condition is how I earn a living. It was all about "in network" and "out of network." What was allowed and not allowed. Being a WNBA player had nothing to do with it. It was a dollars and cents choice made by someone who didn't know me, or my situation. All that mattered was that I choose an "in network" surgeon if I wanted the surgery to be covered.

I was ready for surgery. I was ready for the pain of rehab. I was ready for the struggles during recovery. I wasn't ready for this! At this point I was pretty floored!

I couldn't understand why I'd been sent to a doctor that they said was one of the best in the country and yet when it was time to have surgery, I wasn't able to use him. There is clearly something wrong with this system...but that is for someone else to deal with.

So after I got mad, had tears, and was ready to lose my mind, suddenly a peace came over me. I realized that, like the insurance companies, I had to approach this like business. Becoming CEO of me! When your body is your business you have to approach it like that. Get a new game plan and prepare to execute. Me being healthy and able to play is positive for the success of the team as well. But the reality is the Health Care industry doesn't see class or ethnicity, they see one thing - the bottom line. So instead of getting mad, I educated myself. That is one of the greatest weapons a person can have. Gaining knowledge that helps you grow and be able to share with other athletes, business people and children.

I had another tough decision to make. The team offered for me to come back to Seattle and have the surgery with the back specialist there. My agents and I felt like it would be best to get a doctor not affiliated with the team or league to perform the surgery on me. Now don't take this the wrong way; I didn't think our team doctors were bad or anything along those lines. I just didn't want something to come up and there was a conflict of interest or pressure on them or me based on how my body reacted for my return. I wanted to be free and clear of that.

My agents and I decided that it was best for me to seek out another doctor to have the surgery performed. And the first thing that came to mind was going back home, home to my doctors from high school and college in Pittsburgh. They always say: no matter what happens you can always return home. So I called up Brian Hagen Ph.D. PT at UMPC Center of Sports Medicine. Brian has always looked out for my best interest for years so it was only right he be the one to help me find the right doctor. And help me find a doctor he did. I'd received treatment from them in the past and I loved their work and their professionalism. They had some of the top doctors as well so I felt like it would be best for me to go with them. I knew I'd get the best possible treatment available to me at the time. He connected me with Doctor J. Maroon a top neurosurgeon for the Pittsburgh Steelers. Brian told me not to worry about the insurance stuff, they would take care of me and for the first time in a while I felt like I was home. Doctor Maroon and his staff moved swiftly to schedule my appointment after getting through all the insurance red tape.

March 9th came and it was time for my surgery. I was nervous and scared but all smiles because I had loved ones around me. It's amazing what a difference it can make to have a support system around you when you are going through something like surgery.

Dr. Maroon came before the surgery to meet everyone and say hello. He was so funny, cracking jokes about him being a runner etc. Next thing I know I closed my eyes and when they opened it was all done. The pain was gone…or it might have been the drugs I was on. But I felt my strength renewed. Even if I didn't play one more game, this decision was worth it.

The Recovery

My surgery was in March of 2009. The doctor let me know that it could take up to 4-6 months to be fully healed before I'd be back on the court. That wasn't acceptable for me. I had to be better than that. I let the doctor know that I was going to hit this rehab hard as if my whole career depended on it. I declared this was my grind season. We were in the off-season for the WNBA but I had to treat it like it was my only season and nothing else mattered. I didn't want to miss a single game of the 2009 season and I was ready and willing to work my butt off to get back to where I'd fallen from because of this back injury and foolishness. Hard work and dedication would have to become my best friends. No excuses and no explanations. I had to make it back by any means necessary. I've seen some people get injured and decide to milk it and use it as a break and they never came back the same. I didn't want that to be me. In fact it couldn't be me. I had to be better than average and even good wasn't good enough. I needed a great recovery.

I immediately thought back to my UCONN days and I remembered the work I'd put in with my strength and conditioning coach Andrea Hudy. She was one to watch and one of the best in the country at what she did. If I had to choose who would have me back faster and better, that would be Andrea Hudy. Talk about excellence. As a freshmen at UCONN, I thought she was nuts! lol By my senior year I realized her tough love helped me find that mental edge within. She pushes players to another realm and demands greatness and nothing else. She's the best and I needed the best - point blank, period.

I gave Hudy (as everyone calls her) a call and told her about my situation and that I needed to come work with her. She said: come on out here Swin and you can even stay with me if you want. I felt so blessed that she would give of her time and open her house to me. I was so thankful. But I had one tiny little problem. Well, actually two very big hairy problems. Andrea has two enormous dogs! I mean gigantic, colossal, horse-sized dogs! Now to say I have a fear of dogs would probably be an understatement. I can handle little dogs, but big dogs…well, not so much. Thankfully, Andrea understood my issue.

However, I knew I had to figure something out. I was talking to my close friend Tamika Raymond, who I played with at UCONN and she now coached at Kansas, and she told me to give Lew Perkins a call. See Tamika had already spoken to Lew so they all were in on helping me get back on my feet. Talk about extended family! So I called Lew Perkins, he was the Athletic Director at UCONN when I was there. During this time, he was the Athletic Director at Kansas. This was becoming the perfect situation. I told Lew that I was thinking about coming out there and before I could ask him, he told me that he'd heard about it from Andrea and Tamika and that I needed to come stay with him and his wife Gwen. But Lew had a huge dog named Benson. (Hmmmm, I really need to get over this phobia…) Ever-thoughtful Lew, kindly opened his home to me and assured me that Benson had his own area of the house so I wouldn't ever see him. He told me that I could also use one of their cars while I was there. Could it be written any sweeter than that? God sent me a blessing on a silver platter. It was like He was assuring me that He was still by my side and that everything would be ok. My UCONN family came through for me and it touched my heart. I'm forever thankful to Andrea, Lew, Gwen and my sis Tamika. Without their grace I'm not sure how I would've recovered and certainly not in the fashion that I did.

I flew into Kansas ready to get to work. Andrea didn't disappoint. In fact she surprised me. She took me to a level I'd never been before. She kicked my butt. She worked me as if I was coming in at 100% and wanted to go to 120%. She didn't cut any corners and she didn't give me any breaks to feel sorry for myself; not that I would have anyways. She had me doing all kinds of stuff. She even brought in a boxing trainer to do boxing workouts. It was something to see. We went to a heightened level and operated in that space for three months.

I owe so much to the people who looked out for me while I was in Kansas getting me back to my playing level. I couldn't have done it without them.

The Comeback Begins

On June 3rd I was cleared to play so I packed up my bags and heading to the Seattle. It only took me 3 months to get back in action. The work I'd put in with Andrea paid off and it was go-time! I only missed one preseason game so I was right on time. I got right to it and my journey began, back to claiming my spot on the next Olympic team. I was counting every step and every accomplishment as a sign in my progress.

In the 2009 season I was chosen to be in the All-Star game. It's hard to explain this feeling because I'd just come back from back surgery four months earlier and now I was being called to play in the All-Star game in Connecticut. It was a great feeling. It was like the light at the end of the tunnel. What a reward to be able to come back and make that much of an impact to be named an All-Star after all I'd just gone through.

On top of that, the next blessing was that the game was in Connecticut where I'd played college ball. Some of my teammates from college were also playing in the game so it was like a homecoming for us. I was so excited because my mom and family would be able to come. Everyone was there, so there wasn't a better feeling than to know that I'd get to play in front of a home crowd. I had been tested but now I was seeing the rewards; the rainbow after the rain. It was a great feeling.

It was game time in Connecticut and I got on the floor and went to another zone. I've seen All-Star games where players just have fun but don't play full out. But something just came over me. I could do nothing other than play my heart out. It was like I had a pair of invisible Angel wings on my back. I felt so good out there. I was hitting shots, grabbing boards, dishing assists. I was in tune with my body, my team and the crowd – it felt amazing! I put all of myself into that game for my family and friends that were in the stands and even on the court. I sent a little message to everyone, including myself, that I was back and I had a blast doing it.

Then after the game we had to wait for them to name the MVP. The next thing you know, I hear my name called and I was so elated. That was truly the icing on the cake. To have my loved ones in the stands and even my strength and conditioning coach Andrea Hudy had flown in to see the game. Words can't really describe it. A few months ago I needed know what the future held but through my faith, family, and true supporters I was standing here in this moment with the best players in the world. Seriously, I had just received the MVP award after just having back surgery four months ago. Wow! Speechless! I couldn't have written it better myself. Only the big guy upsets can write a story like that. I was touched. They gave me the microphone and I thanked so many people. My blood was rushing and my thoughts were going a mile a minute and I was so in the moment. Everything I wanted to say I didn't and everyone I wanted to thank I didn't. It was a very overwhelming experience.

After my speech was over and I reflected on it, my stomach started to hurt really badly. I had a gut-wrenching feeling because I'd forgotten to thank Lew Perkins and his wife Gwen. They'd done so much for me and opened up their home to me and rolled out the red carpet. They gave me a little sanctuary. I couldn't have done it without them. No matter what they had going on at their house with students or whomever they always made sure that my space was ok and I was taken care of. They treated me so well and really looked out for me and I forgot to thank them while I was on the mic.

In that moment I blew it, so to Lew and Gwen Perkins I'm thanking you publicly now. What you did for me meant everything and I'll never forget it.

No one is an island. No matter who you are or where you want to go in life it will always take others to help you get there. I really have a lot of people to thank for being there for me and supporting me. I was fighting back and it was a long road but because of the love and support around me I was able to keep going. I was learning on this journey in the low and the high points. While I was in the valley and while I was on the climb I was always learning. It took a lot of dedication, persistence, and perseverance to do what I desired to do but I set out to do it and with the unbelievable support of others, I was able to achieve what even I could not have imagined.

Our season went on after that and we kept fighting and trying to make something happen. One of our star players went down with an injury though and that hurt us pretty badly. I was finally back and feeling good and then someone other than me was hurt so we still couldn't do all that we wanted to do. I wanted so badly to have a fully healthy team but it just wasn't in the hand we were dealt. We were eliminated in the first round again and we went home with the hopes that we could do better the next year. There were a lot of lessons to learn in defeat but in order to learn how to win we must learn how to take a loss. I couldn't hang my head low though because I'd given all that I could and we came up short. The key is that you always have to do the best you can and you'll never regret giving your all.

The China Experience

After the 2009 season my focus grew more and more on getting back to the Olympics, which was my main goal and I had to continue to better myself, and my game so I would be ready. We don't plan to fail, we fail to plan. I had to make a plan of action and carry it out. I realized that with my body and what I'd been through that I could no longer play year round like a lot of other ladies did. It was very normal to play an entire WNBA season and then go overseas and play another 6-7 months and then come home and start right back playing in the WNBA. It was a year round grind that can take a toll on your body. I had to play smart. I had to find the right second job that would allow my game to grow, would give me court time but would also not subject my body to such a long season.

I sat down to game plan with my agents and we came up with the idea that I'd play in China. China has a pretty good league but their season is shorter. So instead of playing 6-7 months I'd play 3-4 months. I felt like my body could handle that load and I'd be able to have some financial security while staying active, then come home and get a little rest before the season started back up in the WNBA.

I had never been to China and had no clue what China would be like. My agent tried to prepare me but I didn't understand fully what I was getting into. Many American players try to play in China but end up coming home early because they feel too isolated. It's an entirely different world from where we live. Not to say one is better than the other just to say that my views are different because I was raised in a different culture.

I was playing in southern China in a city called Guangzhou. Everything was different including the way we traveled. Over there we could have five-hour bus rides on a very small bus. In America if you take a bus it's usually a big charter bus that can be more comfortable. But in China and parts of Europe the buses are smaller and so are the roads you travel on.

Over there we were in a very small bus because everything is made smaller in some of the more rural areas. But while in some of the major cities we had a big bus, which my 6ft 11inch teammate could appreciate. Sometimes we would fly for four hours and then ride on a little bus for another five hours. It was very different and very trying. It definitely tested my mental fortitude, in a way like never before.

Another interesting thing was that their teams could only have one American player. I'm assuming that they didn't want the foreign players to come over and take playing time away from the Chinese players. Which I would eventually grow to understand, they wanted players to develop, which comes from playing. Needless to say I was the only American on the team and only person that spoke English other than me was translator Delphee. I would come to learn later that some of my teammates spoke some English but were shy like Yao Ming used to be when he first came to the NBA. Delphee was very cool, he was my only relief for awhile and he made it a little easier for me while I was over there. Of course it was a culture shock at first because it was so new and different. Although sometimes I did feel bad that Delphee would have to go to shopping with me for things that most husbands would never want to be bothered with! I started learning some basic words after that.

Delphee understood some of the American culture and he loved the NBA so we would talk about games and players all the time. There is nothing more special than having someone you can laugh and talk with; I really needed that. He would take me to Hong Kong and to McDonalds and really helped me experience a little bit of America when I needed a fix. I was a 45-minute train ride from Hong Kong and I would go there maybe once or twice a month to shop, see some cool sites and speak English with a lot of the Brits that lived there. Hong Kong is owned by China but they let them keep their own flavor. In Hong Kong there aren't the same Internet restrictions as there is in China. In Hong Kong there are American restaurants and it almost has a mini New York feel to it. I'd go there and hit the reset button. It helped. It was all relatively new so in all fairness to the mainland of China I hadn't learned a lot about its culture.

It was very tough being restricted in so many ways. Because of my diet, which consists of no pork, having a proper balance of nutrients was tough. I also couldn't just get online and go to my favorite websites. I couldn't even tweet! You know how hard that must have been for me. (Thankfully I set up a Weibo account – which is the equivalent of twitter in China.) It was one of the most humbling experiences that I've ever had to go through. The players on my team were of course used to it but it was challenging for me in a way that I didn't expect. It made me a better person I feel though. I really began to grow closer with my teammates. I got out of my comfort zone and into an effective zone.

My past tests and lessons had taught me enough to know how to adapt, so I began to buy into the system and I started wanting to learn more about them and their culture. My teammates were so surprised and it made them like me a lot because never before had they been around a foreign player that was so interested in learning about their culture and learning their language and their way of life. For a lot of them it was also their first time interacting with an African American woman. Most of them only knew of Africans that had come to China from Africa. They didn't know that there were different types of black people so it was a learning experience for them as well. I tried to teach them as much about my culture as I could. I showed them the different haircuts and hairstyles that I'd get and all about my hair. They learned more about Christmas and I remember them getting me Christmas gifts to make me feel at home. They taught me about the Chinese New Year and I celebrated it with them by getting them gifts. I'd teach them words in English and they'd teach me words in Chinese. We began bonding and laughing with one another. I think we both learned about the beauties of one another's culture and we all grew from the experience. It was a test and a testament. It tested my ability to adapt to a new situation and learn and grown from it and it was a testament to the human spirit. Friends can be created no matter the differences. You need only make the effort to understand and appreciate one another.

It was also like my wilderness in another aspect. In the Bible you read of people that go into the wilderness to be ministered to; well, this is what it was like for me. In my apartment I couldn't do anything but sit and think. I could watch limited TV and I couldn't surf the Internet completely so there was nothing to do but get to know myself better. It was a healing experience that words almost can't explain. It took me to a peaceful place where my mind grew clearer and more conscious of the things around me and of the beauty and complexities of life. It was a spiritual cleanse that I desperately needed but didn't know it prior to heading over there.

I found clarity in China and I grew as a woman. I got back to my spiritual roots and rediscovered my faith and my foundation. I thought a lot about who I was as a woman and as a basketball player and what I really wanted out of life. It's very important that we get to know ourselves and that we get in a quiet place and grow. China did more for me than I did for China.

I can honestly say that. No matter what you're going through or where you're at in your life I guarantee you that if you look close enough there's some beauty in that struggle. There's a blessing in that lesson. Don't look at your situation for all that it isn't; look at your situation for all that it is. I once heard someone say: It's in the valley where I grow. Now I know what they meant by that. In those low and quiet places is where you'll find your growth. Embrace it.

My team and I grew close in China and we played as hard as we could. We got knocked out in the first round of the playoffs and we walked off with our heads held high. Those ladies were a blessing to be around. They even took losses in a positive way. They were just grateful for the opportunity to play and they didn't ever mope or complain. Playing basketball was a luxury to them, not a birthright. I will always be thankful to them and for them.

I had a blast but it was time for me to head back to the states and get back into my US groove.

The Storybook Season

I made it back to the states in February of 2010 and I was ready to get back into basketball in the WNBA. I felt so different this time. I was refreshed. I was focused. My mind was clear. I was stronger and I wanted more out of life. China gave me so much time to reflect on my life and what I wanted that now I was ready to take my life back. I wanted to clean out the clutter in my life and be in control of my destiny. I still had some issues in my personal life and relationship space that I needed to work on. I was headed in that direction. It was time for a change. I'd figured out what I wanted and now it was getting close to the time to take action.

I got back to the team and we started camp. There was a different aura in the gym this time around. I could feel the energy had shifted. I know what I'd been through and the growth I had but I didn't know what everyone else had learned over their time away from the WNBA. I could tell something was going on though and I wanted to find out more about this feeling I was having. We had a couple new faces on the team including one very familiar to me. My UCONN teammate Svetlana Abrosimova decided to return to the WNBA after sitting out the 2009 season and became a key contributor off the bench. Our other new face, Lecoe Willingham, also came off the bench to give us the depth we needed to make a serious run in the playoffs and get past our recent first-round rut.

On the court we were getting after it pretty hard. We were intense and there was a sense of urgency on the floor that I could feel. We'd had two bad seasons prior to this and we hadn't played a full season with everyone healthy and this time around we wanted that to be different. We had what it took to be the best in the league and if you looked at the roster you wouldn't be able to understand how we weren't already. We wanted a different outcome to this season and we were ready and willing to put in the work to make it happen. Everyone elevated their game and their attitude.

Off the court we were different as well. We had a growth spurt mentally, emotionally, and spiritually and it was evident. I remember there was a group of ladies that came together and decided to have a Bible study once a week with our chaplains. We were going to utilize the chaplains and make this season about more than basketball. We realized that everything affects everything so if your personal life is out of sync then that will have a trickle-down effect on your game. It was Tanisha Wright, Ashley Robinson, Camille Little, and myself. We came together and we bonded and made an agreement that we wouldn't let negativity in, but that we would build one another up and pray for one another. To quietly let faith be our guide in this season. We all were imperfect but we respected each other and accepted each other's flaws and all! No judgment, no jury, just love! We incorporated our faith and that spirit affected everyone on the team whether they knew it or not. Positivity is just as contagious as negativity. You just have to choose which one you're going to spread. By us remaining focused and keeping our balance we were able to balance as a team. The positive mentality spread through our whole team and there was a chain reaction to this new positive attitude. We weren't individuals; we were a team. I'm sure our coaching staff was elated to see this transformation and this new team unit healthy mentally and physically and ready to go. I'm sure that's a coach's dream and the change came from within. The change wasn't from the top down. The change came from the players who decided to do this one differently and that affected everything around us.

Basketball is a mental game so if your mind is on right then your game begins to click on all cylinders. We were clicking and we were winning. There was a powerhouse type of vibe that our team had that year and we walked in it. We went on winning streaks like none other and we enjoyed every minute of it. Each win is a little more encouraging than the one before. Each win made us a little bit stronger. It made us so strong that even if a loss was sprinkled in, it didn't affect us much. There was a camaraderie that showed on the court and resulted in wins. When all was said and done we rewrote the record books for both Seattle sports and the WNBA. We finished with the highest winning percentage in Seattle sports history and, among others, tied the record for most wins in WNBA regular season history.

The All-Star break was coming up for us but this year it was going to be different because it was the World Championships year. The FIBA World Championships are every two years and the Olympics are every four years. This year instead of a normal All-Star game they wanted the US National Team to play against the WNBA All-Stars. I received a call to be a part of the US National Team. I was very excited about this opportunity and I took it as a sign. In my mind I saw it as getting one step closer to my goal of being on the 2012 Olympic team. I'm not sure if that's the message they were trying to send me but that's how I took it, nonetheless. I played in that game over our All-Star break and it was fun and very much worth it.

After that was over in July, it was time for us to get back to our regular schedule and start back winning again. We came together as a team and we agreed to give it our all and to do it like we've never done before. For the first time we were all healthy and it would be my first time playing a full season with Lauren Jackson and I was excited about that. Lauren can really play the game of basketball so having her healthy meant a lot to us as a team. Plus I was loving her new fire red hair; new "do", new team… "let's get it!", is what I say! We banded together and we got serious and the results showed up. We were kicking butts and taking names. The more we won the stronger we got.

Then came the playoffs. We were very serious this playoff run and we didn't intend to let anyone stand in our way of our ultimate goal. We buckled down and locked in and played our hearts out. Every play was played like it could be the game winning play. There wasn't any arguing, fighting, and pointing fingers. We were a unit and we played as such. We were selfless and sacrificed our bodies for the ball. If there was a loose ball we wanted it. If there was a bad play we let it go and looked to the next one. If anyone was struggling we cheered her back into the game. We didn't let anyone fall. We picked everyone up and we held one another up every game. Our bench was just as strong as the players on the floor. They didn't sit and look; they were engaged. We clapped it up and cheered for one another all game long. It was business but it was a pleasure also. This is how basketball is meant to be played.

It was the storybook season. The electricity in the arena in Seattle was unreal. We went on to sweep the playoffs becoming the first time in WNBA history to be undefeated at home on our way to winning the 2010 WNBA championship. What a year! We came, we saw, we conquered. Everything we set out to do, we did it. For me it couldn't have been any sweeter.

This was my 3rd WNBA Championship. Yes! I was the 2nd player that had won a WNBA Championship in the East and in the West, and I was the 1st to start on both teams. But this redemption brought tears of pure joy. Sometimes when you are in the thick of things you tend to forget some of the amazing things you've been able to accomplish. But in that moment, my heart and my soul just felt so overwhelmingly grateful.

It was a crazy feeling after we won. I was running all over. My teammates were all over the place. I ran up and hugged my mom. She had this huge smile on her face like a proud momma would. It was an amazing feeling. This one felt completely different than the others because of all that I'd been through. I remember being on the podium and tears began to roll down my eyes and I looked up to God and said, THANK YOU! I had to thank God because he'd brought me through so much since 2008 when I started this journey to get back to the Gold. I felt like God was telling me: I told you everything would be ok and that it'll all work out in your favor. I remember one of the Storm owners Lisa hugging me and say I'm so proud of you, you deserve it and all I could do was smile. It's like everything was in slow motion, so magical and the aura was soothing.

I flashed back to crying on the couch in my apartment when I got the call saying that I didn't make the

2008 Olympic team. I remembered the surgery and the drama with that. I remembered the work I put in to get healthy. I remember the All-Star game and being named MVP. I thought about China and how I'd grown so much in just a few months over there. It all flashed in that moment and it felt so good.

China had taught me so much about myself and brought me to a place where I was so strong and stable. I was in a space in my life that even if we hadn't won the championship I would've been fine because of the journey we had that year. We had such an amazing team that year and it was such a special experience that it would've been just fine had we not won the Championship. The Championship was the icing on the cake and the reward at the end of a hard race. That was an experience that year that I'll never forget. It was such a healing experience. I worked on myself inwardly and was rewarded outwardly. Those are the types of feelings you live for. I'd only been on a team like that a couple times in my life and it was just as special this time around. Things were looking good for me at the moment and I was proud of everything I'd made it through.

It didn't stop there though. Before I could let the win marinate I received a call along with my teammate Sue Bird. They told us that there was a two-day training session in the Czech Republic and that after that they were going to pick the US National Team for the World Championships. This was a huge call for me in more ways than one. I was honored that they were inviting me because it was another step towards my goal. I knew that if I went it would be a big risk though. That's a long flight and a huge step to go try out and then not make the team. As you remember, I'd sacrificed in the past to make the US Olympic team and was let down. Naturally that thought crossed my mind but I couldn't turn down this opportunity. When you want something you have to be willing to go after it no matter what stands in between you and your goal. I've always heard that anything worth having is worth sacrificing for, so this is a sacrifice I wanted to make. Sue was the starting point guard for the US National Team already so it was kind of a given that she'd make the team. I was on my own in this gamble, but I had to take it anyways.

The way it was set up was that if we swept Atlanta then we'd have to fly back to Seattle, have two days in Seattle to get ready, and then we'd have to catch a flight over to the Czech Republic. It was a very tight schedule, which added to the intensity of this moment.

It was amazing winning the championship and celebrating with my teammates, Nate, our practice players, and all our fans. Unfortunately Sue and I would wake up the next morning and now it was time to focus on joining Team USA in Prague. I had less than 24 hours to pack everything in my apartment in Seattle before my flight. Have you ever packed up an apartment? Imagine having to do it in less than 24 hours! (Cue Mission Impossible music...)

In times like this I could always depend on my girls. No not my teammates although I love them, but my Seattle ball girls Aimee, Jaulane and Marissa. I had a special bond with them since I arrived in Seattle. If anyone would help get me packed up it would be those young ladies. There's nothing like music, pizza, packing and reminiscing. Needless to say I made that flight to Prague with Sue and, like always, my loves came through for me.

Off to Prague

Thanks to the girls, I made the trip to Prague and was ready to handle business over there. I landed and I went straight to work for those two days. I bust my butt and left everything on the floor. It was all that I could give and the opportunity was all that I could ask for. I was grateful to even be in the pool of players. There were a lot of talented players there so it was kind of up in the air. One thing in my favor was that I'd just become a Champion, so I was flying in there with that title. I don't think it meant too much but it was a momentum thing. I was feeling good, playing well, and in a very solid space in my life.

After the tryouts, they set up some time to call each of us in the coach's room. I was nervous when it was my turn but I knew that I'd done all that I could do. In the room were Carol Callan and Coach Auriemma. Coach Auriemma was my college coach so I was familiar with him and his style. He asked me in his usual sarcastic voice did I think I deserved to be on this team. I answered him in my sarcastic voice with a sharp yes. He chuckled a little and then asked me why. I told him that I felt I brought a lot to the team and that I worked hard and showed what I can do and that I deserve a shot. He shook his head and said that he agreed and that I made the team. What a relief. The trip was not in vain. I stood up and hugged them both and thanked them kindly and went on my way. I ran to my room and called my mom to tell her the good news. I was very happy and I wanted to keep my family up to speed with all my happenings. They saw my struggle and my grind and I wanted them to see that this was finally coming together.

I'd made it! It was another step in the right direction. I was on my way and I kept getting sign after sign that I was on the right path and operating in the right space in my life. I took a risk and it paid off. It taught me another lesson in life. Always go after what you want and never give up. The task may look daunting but if you attack it with a willing heart, focused mind, and a positive attitude you will achieve what you set out to do. I could have told myself that this sacrifice would turn out just like the one did in 2008. I could have told myself that it wasn't my ultimate goal so this step wasn't necessary or worth the trouble. I could've told myself that I needed some rest because of my back and that I needed time with my family to have fun after my Championship win. There were a lot of excuses that I could have made out of fear of failure but I decided not to and look how it turned out. It worked in my favor and I'm glad I took the risk. I encourage you to do the same for your dream.

The World Championships were shaping up to be a great experience. I love the fact that I was a UCONN Husky in college because this team was almost like a UCONN reunion. Or so they say lol. I'm sure most people won't like to hear that but oh well. I mean let's be real, Tina Charles and Maya Moore were watching Sue, Asjha and I while they were in high school. We all went to the same school but totally different eras. It felt so good after coming off of a Championship and then to roll right into this with my Seattle teammate Sue. Then in addition to playing with Sue Bird there was Tamika Catchings and Diana Taurasi. It reminded me of our 2004 Olympic team and it's what I was dreaming of in 2008. It didn't happen for me but now here I was playing with them all again. It was an amazing feeling to see how life comes full circle and how opportunities come back around to those who are diligent and steadfast.

The UCONN brand was heavy on this team. There was our Coach Geno Auriemma. Then there were my girls Asjha Jones, Diana Taurasi, Sue Bird, myself, and then some younger UCONN ladies like Tina Charles and Maya Moore. That amazed me and I was in love with the moment. I love being surrounded by greatness. We had an amazing time in the Czech Republic. We weren't counting our minutes or our stats we just played hard day in and day out. There was so much laughter and so much fun going on between us. Our family that came over loved it and had a great time and we would go after it every time we stepped on the court. We were a stacked team and definitely a force to reckon with.

I was honored to be a part of such a special team. My focus was on having a great time and staying ready so that when my number was called I could go out on the court and have an impact. I stayed ready and cheered my team on. Everyone has always known me to be an impact player and as that player that could get in a game and make some big plays. It was all about heart and hustle. That's what I was known for and that's the mentality that I was sticking to. I remember there was a game we were playing in and I was on the bench the first half and then coach told me that I'd be starting the second half. I was ready to go. I got in the game and went hard! I was able to help change up the tempo in the game. We were pressing and getting after them. It felt so divine being out there and I was so happy to be on the floor doing what I do best. Our energy was up and we won the game. We kept winning and became the World Champions.

Now not only had I just won the WNBA Championship but also I went over to Czech Republic made the team and then won the FIBA World Championship. 2010 was an amazing year to say the least. The accolades were racking up for us and it felt so good to be on that journey back to where I wanted to be. I knew that I couldn't get complacent because at any given time there could be a bump in the road but I stayed positive and kept moving forward with my life.

Halftime

Letting Go of Toxic Relationships

There comes a time when you have to evaluate your life and be honest with yourself. You must ask yourself if the people in your life are building you up or tearing you down. For several different reasons we allow certain people to come into our lives and sometimes we also allow those people to stay longer than they are supposed to. It's important that we recognize when someone's time is up. That time is usually when the bad outweighs the good and we are no longer being lifted up but instead being weighed down. If you picture a climb to the top of a mountain and imagine carrying someone else's body weight on your back that climb becomes very cumbersome even just to imagine. Well, imagine having to actually do it day in and day out. It's nearly impossible to reach your goals if you're carrying excess baggage along the way. You have to remove all toxic people from your life so that you can truly live your life to your fullest potential. And though we all can look around and instinctively know who needs to go, going through with the "surgery" to remove them from your life can be more difficult than going through cancer. I know both from experience. But it doesn't mean you can't or shouldn't do it. I believe the most courageous people – the strongest people – are the ones who are able to remove toxic people from their lives.

I'd like to speak to my diehard romantics on this one. We all want love in some form or another. Most of us dream about having that Cinderella wedding and being whisked away into a land of love and living out our days with our Prince Charming. We want someone to make us feel beautiful, appreciated, respected, cherished, and most of all, loved. It's a dream that we have from the age of boy awareness. From the time we understand what a boyfriend or girlfriend is until the time that we understand what a life partner is we desire this type of love. One issue is that most of us may not know exactly what love looks like although we are subconsciously looking for it. If you don't know what it looks like then something will appear and you'll accept it and you may not realize the difference until it's too late. I used to think love was very simple; you love me I love you then happily ever after. Well love is not! It can be complicated, layered and at times challenging. I want to forewarn you so that from this day forward you're aware of what you're attracting and of the people in your life. This isn't about bashing people or categorizing them all together. It's about your own self-worth, respect and happiness.

I learned a lot of lessons on this journey of mine and one of the major ones had to do with love, or should I say toxic love. I was hesitant to talk about this topic because I've enjoyed my privacy the last few years. But I read so many stories about people, especially women, who made bad choices that I felt my lesson could possibly save young women or men this kind of pain. I had no choice. I needed to tear open my wounds and reveal my scars caused by the acid of toxic relationships. Although my humble journey had seen unspeakable lows and exhilarating highs, there was always an undercurrent. That undercurrent was dragging me down and I didn't even know it. Or maybe I just didn't want to…

My mind takes me back to a relationship I had that became very unhealthy and toxic. Early on there were good times and many smiles and laughter, but there was an overall feeling that didn't feel quite as good. Slowly I began to lose who I was. The toxicity of this relationship I found myself in began to eat away at my core and started to change my outlook on life. I was being broken down and trained to be someone else's footstool instead of being lifted up and loved the way I deserved. The more I hurt the more love I gave. I was hoping that if I loved more, gave more, and sacrificed more that eventually it would be given back to me in that same form. To my surprise I was proven wrong. The love never came back the way I sent it out. Instead I received a form of hate that was labeled as love. I accepted it for a long time not realizing I was making it worse because I was reinforcing it. By reinforcing it I mean I would stay even after a horrible argument. I would go and buy him a nice gift because I knew it would make him smile and at least keep the peace for a while. I no longer recognized who I had become. Why did I stay, why did I love him so much, why did I make excuses for a lot of his actions? I started trying to live up to someone else's expectations in this world and that person didn't give me life nor did he hold my future. I put it in his hands though and I gave him my power. I even distanced myself from friends and loved ones to please this person and I shut out the prominent voices that could have spoken change into my life. The same positive voices that got me to where I was were now being shut out while I tried to carry out this toxic relationship. How was I smiling in front of family, friends, colleagues and the world but feeling like I was drowning on the inside? Slowly losing my faith, slowly losing my mind, and living like I was walking on eggshells every time he was around. It was like a roller coaster and I had no idea how to get off. I thought I could fix it. I was naïve, gullible and so out of character.

They say the first year you are dating that person's representative then the second year you meet their true self and in this case they were right. I remember always thinking back to the first year and telling myself how great he was, and much he loved me and that we could find our way back to that place. But the reality is you can't when you're not being honest about who you are, expectations and goals aren't clear. That's what happens when we are blinded by "love." It's not love at all but we call it that.

I'm sure any doctor will tell you that when you're injured and trying to heal, stress isn't a good thing to be dealing with. I learned that a lot of the pain in my body could have been made worse by all of the relationship stress that I was dealing with. Relationship stress is one of the worse types of stress a person can have. It prolongs your injuries and sicknesses and it decreases your life expectancy. Our life literally depends on the love we receive. Love is the greatest gift given to man by God and it cannot be taken lightly. We must learn to love and allow only genuine love in our lives. Don't be tricked into giving yourself to someone that isn't giving anything back to you. Don't be what your partner tells you to be, be who God has called you to be. Don't let anyone spew his or her self-hate onto you and call it love.

I wasn't being loved in this relationship the way a woman is supposed to be loved. I received "love" but mostly when people were around. When it was time to smile for the cameras or pretend to family and friends. It was all for show. I realized after I'd come from China that I had to clean up my life. I had to get everyone that wasn't adding to my life out of my life. You have givers and you have takers. We must all strive to be givers and then everyone will be forever receiving. Don't get stuck in a place that you are so desperate for love that you accept anyone and everything and just label it as love. You have to realize when you and that person aren't compatible. Don't try to fit a square peg into a circular hole! It's not going to happen. I saw him have signs of being loving, caring, and compassionate, but those times never amount to the level of stress from the bad times.

In any relationship you should never feel controlled and made to feel near worthless nor manipulated and coerced. That means in your personal, business or professional relationships. It's easy to look back in hindsight but you have to see signs while you are in it. You have to trust that subconscious and stay connected to the foundation of who you are. No matter what face I tried to put on I knew that deep down I wasn't happy. I had to walk away. And when I did, that was a sign because everything started going right in my life.

You have to have the faith to walk away. So many people get stuck in a place that they are so afraid to leave because they've gotten used to it. You have to trust that everything will be ok. It's not the end if you leave that situation. It's actually just the beginning. I left that toxic relationship during this journey and after I did I felt so much better. I found peace. There was a peace in my life that surpassed all understanding. My life felt so much better and I felt truly free. Things began to go right and I could tell that I'd done the right thing concerning this relationship.

I want you to know that just because your partner doesn't physically put their hands on you doesn't necessarily mean they aren't abusing you. If you're constantly angry or turning into someone you don't recognize, pack up them bags and walk on! When someone emotionally or verbally abuses you that can affect you just as severely. You must always be aware and forever learning so that if you see the red flags of verbal or physical abuse you can recognize them and take action.

I remember being so blinded in my toxic love that others didn't even feel comfortable approaching me with advice. I was making excuses in my mind for him and blaming myself. I was questioning myself and wondering what I did wrong to get to this point. I take some of the blame not for his actions but for my inaction. I blame myself for being afraid to fail and for not listening to my Grandma when she taught me to always stand on faith. I dealt with so much at the time but I always tried to keep a smile on my face, to hide the pain in my heart. It's not fun feeling like you're being put down and critiqued constantly. From the clothes you wear, to your faith, to the friends you keep. It makes you feel horrible about yourself. Eventually you start to feel inferior and unworthy. I found myself always buying gifts trying to keep the peace or apologizing just so we could stop the foolishness and get along. You probably want to throw up now, trust me I did too while writing this. Unfortunately the strongest women, most educated, most beautiful you name it, all have and can go through a lot of the same things. So I won't put myself on a pedestal and act like I've never gone through this, I just won't. It happened to me. It can happen to anyone.

Looking back I was afraid to leave for some reason. Maybe it was my fear of looking like a failure to so many people around me. I would have easily walked away. But I didn't! I was screaming on the inside but smiling like a beauty queen on the outside. I felt like I was trapped in a burning house and I couldn't get out. I was crying out for help but my mouth wasn't moving. I finally got the courage to leave and then people started to open up to me. What I realized is that they were all speaking the truth. When you think your hiding the pain those closest to you can truly see. Someone will choose to speak up others will choose to just stay prayed up for you.

When you're blinded by "love" you will cut off any and everyone to protect the person you're with. You will isolate yourself from everyone that doesn't approve of your relationship. It's important that your relationship is safe enough that you can keep close friends and family around. You need checks and balances. The people that know and love you and that have been there way before this new person you're with should always feel like they can be honest with you. When the people that truly love you are being shut out of your life that's when you're in trouble.

One of the things I earned from my toxic love was that you should never put your partner on such a high pedestal that you can't take them off. I was holding on to this relationship and living this lie because I had built it up and put it on a pedestal. I was afraid to leave and be seen as a failure. I didn't know if it was my competitive nature or my disdain for losing. Whatever it was, I had trapped myself. But there is no trap that can keep you in chains. Only insecurity and fear keep you there! Faith and desire for a renewed heart and clear mind can begin to set you free.

When you're dealing with a toxic relationship, you usually have what I like to call a Walk On moment. Think about Angela Bassett in Waiting to Exhale after she set the car on fire. Now I'm not saying burn anything! But you have to admit when she strutted away from that burning car sister girl meant business. Taking your confidence back, your power and joy is the most invigorating thing. That's when you realize I'm worth it. This last story always makes me laugh because it depicts the foolish heights we let this toxic love go. One afternoon he and I were in the airport and headed to our gate. I stopped at a newsstand and got a magazine, cranberry juice, and some candy. I wanted to have something to read on the plane and my favorite light snack. When I got back to where he was standing he looked at me with disgust and asked me why did I need to stop and get a magazine, juice, and candy. He stated that I could have simply drunk the free drink and ate the peanuts they give you on the plane. He said that I was so wasteful with my money and bought unnecessary things. He went on to say that every time I come to the airport I buy a drink for no reason.

I was so blown away that he was questioning me about why I spent less than $10 of my own money on a few things that I wanted. He continued to say how that's a problem for him because if we got married I would be constantly wasting money. Before I responded I remember looking at him from head to toe with his diamond watch, designer outfit and pricy shoes. Then I distinctly remember thinking to myself those were all expensive things I purchased him! They were gifts, each one given for different reasons, but he had no problem accepting them. I was being loving then but "wasteful" now! I've been poor so I know how to watch my money. In fact, I am still very diligent with what I spend, so I thought, "This can't be real life! That foolishness did not just come out this man's mouth!"

I just shook my head because at this point I realized our issue had nothing to do with hard earned money I spent on snacks. What I thought was once love had become completely toxic. We were now wasting each other's time, life and everything else.

I became a much better woman when I owned up to my mistakes and I walked away. I grew in that moment. I learned from that experience and I vowed to never let it happen again. I slowly detoxed that toxic love out of my life but it wasn't easy. He hurt me in more ways than one. Not only because it was over but also because I now had to deal with the reasons why I ever let it happen in the first place.

To my seasoned veterans out there, don't compromise yourself just to have someone in your life. Don't live a lie. Take your time, work on you, and build your life. The right person will appear in your life on God's timing. Just be prepared.

To my young people, focus on you. Don't start out young and searching for love. Find yourself first. Learn from my story and others about what real love is. Know that love doesn't hurt. Love doesn't make you feel bad about yourself. Love doesn't cause tears. If you're going through those things then you aren't being loved and you're with the wrong guy. Let him go and move on with your life. Love yourself first. Perfect you and then you will attract a good guy in due time. No one is worth losing yourself over. No one is worth crying over every day. No one is worth cutting off your friends and family for. Let love be love and stop calling hate, love.

I've learned so much from my mistakes in love. I believe in love, I believe in people and I believe in growth. But I recognize that I will never be the same.

There is a lesson in our mistakes and we have to be wise enough to learn from them. It's time to let go of that toxic love and start healing and preparing for real love to enter your life. I'm stronger now, I'm wiser now but I'm also patient now. Love will find me. I don't need to look for it.

How Love For CFK Helped Fill a Void

One of the greatest relationships I have in my life is with my charity Cash For Kids. I'm married to helping it be a vehicle for young children to get inspired and succeed. Whether it's spending time with the kids in my hometown of McKeesport, PA in our Youth Basketball leagues, or my older kids in the Swin Cash/Youth Places summer league or the kids from Seattle to Chicago, my desire, passion and commitment hasn't wavered. So even when I was at my lowest point, I never neglected what Cash For Kids meant to me or to the kids.

I actually started the basketball leagues in my hometown 3 years ago. I was going through a lot in my personal life but one of the best things I did was reach out and help all our kids in CFK. They needed a league to call their own and I needed their smiles, happiness and laughter just as much. Amazing how your perspective can change when you take the spotlight off of you and everything that's wrong and place it on someone else and see everything that's so pure and right.

Positive People – Positive Influences

Early on in my Seattle days I didn't know many people in the Emerald City. Thank goodness for Nate! Nate worked for the Storm on the game operations crew. I remember how he used to make us all mix CDs. After the game we would come in and they would be in our lockers. He was always doing thoughtful things like that.

Nate and I became closer and he was a big support for me. Being so far from family and friends it was cool to know someone had my back like him. It's rare you find those people that want to help in any way they can but never ask for anything. I remember joking with him about how one day he's going to leave his job and work for my company once we can afford him. He just smiled and said I'm ready when you are.

During our 2010 championship run Nate was right there with our team. He truly was our Sixth Man. Whether it was new music, recommending restaurants or helping me as a friend when I was sick. He's just that type of guy who is always there when you need him. And trust me I appreciated it.

The 2010 season was going better than anyone could have expected. I was in an amazing place space mentally, really building lifelong friendships on my team and it felt like God was positioning me for all he had to come. I talked to my mom everyday on the phone and if I missed a day without calling her she would call and ask if something is wrong. (Nowadays she just laughs and asks me if I'm on a plane because I travel so much.)

But I remember having a conversation with her about ideas I had for Cash for Kids and taking our programming and partnerships to the next level. Mom always has been a big supporter of me giving back to the community. She instilled a work ethic, family values and a sense of giving back in me at a young age. She was overjoyed to see me happy and back to myself. It was hard to hear your Mother say "There were many nights I got down on my knees and prayed for you." I'm sure it's difficult for a parent to watch their child go through pain, but my mom never lost hope or faith. She was now enjoying watching me as I was starting to find myself and focus on the things I loved, like Cash for Kids.

Fast forward a few weeks after that conversation and I met Jakki Nance. Jakki was visiting our team via a program she was presenting for the WNBA about Leaving a Legacy. She was talking about her background and work in the non-profit sector. Right away there was something about her that I liked. She was of course very bubbly, in a room full of tired WNBA players after a hard practice. I remember thinking, bless her heart! I was pumped about her presentation while other teammates informed me not to ask a lot of questions or at least wait and ask her afterwards so they could go shower. Yeah, I was that kid in school that asked questions if I had them and always wanted to know more. So sue me!

Anyways, at the end of Jakki's presentation she offered to help anyone pro bono and to just give her a call. So a few weeks later I did just that. As the season went on, Jakki and I would talk and grow closer. I would later come to realize Jakki and I didn't meet by chance. It was part of a greater plan. She came into my life as I was in a transition period. For me to have another African-American woman that was a lawyer by trade, a wife and a mother who basically said I want to help you not only grow your charity but define who you are to the world was a blessing.

It was hard for me to trust after going through the things I went through but when something feels right, you follow your gut. I mean I had a loving support system already around me spearheaded by my mom. Now Jakki was like another mentor/friend that was helping groom me to be the woman I wanted to become off the court as well as on.

Third Quarter

A New Focus

At the end of 2010 it was time to head back over to China. This time I took a different approach to my trip there. I was going over with my head on straight and I really wanted to capitalize on my time in a country that had so much to offer and where there was so much I could learn.

Last time was a bit of a shock to me but this time I knew what to expect and I knew how I was going to make the most of it. It was time for me to start working more on my brand, dreams, and goals. There are a lot of things I want to do in life so I decided to use my time in China to game plan and begin executing some things while over there. I had visions of Oprah Winfrey and Magic Johnson, and I always had respect for them and wondered what was the road to success for them.

For me, success is defined in terms of happiness, family and the ability to give to others. I spent years dreaming about leaving a great legacy that not only showed success on the court but in all aspects of my life. I wanted to be a great businesswoman, a philanthropist, build a strong brand and of course be a Champion. While in China I could focus on some of these things. I'd removed the toxic people from my life and I was feeling free and clear now. I had an idea about one day starting a denim line for women that are taller than average like myself. I'm really into fashion and a denim line is something I really wanted to do. I realized that practically everything is made in China so why not visit some factories and get some samples made while I'm over there playing? As you can see my mindset was totally different going into China this time than it was last time. I was open and ready for new possibilities. I wanted to begin thinking more about my future and setting myself up for success after basketball. Up until this point my life had been about surviving and just getting by but now that I was growing, my focus was more directed and specific.

Humble Journey

When I arrived in China, I found out that I'd have a new translator. I was pretty sad about that but I was happy for Delphee because he'd gotten a new job and was making more money and doing great. He would still keep in touch and called to check on me from time to time. He also would reach out and let me know what factories to visit while I was there. I was in China not only playing basketball and loving it, but I was handling business off the court. I was visiting factories and getting samples made. I was continuing to dream and to plan and everything was feeling good. I got some text messages here and there from my past but I was so focused on my future that I didn't entertain it. I knew that I couldn't move forward if I was still looking back. The people in your past are there for a reason. You have to realize that and keep going with your life. There was a new guy that came into my life around this time and I'd known him for a long time. We became great friends and he was like a breath of fresh air. There was no pressure and no titles and I just felt free and in a good space. Things were all falling right into place.

Our team was playing great in China and having a lot of fun in the process. Spending time with my teammates in Dongguan, learning more and more about their culture was fascinating. My teammates were more open this year, willing to talk about our similarities, differences and love of music. I know that our countries have philosophical differences but one thing is very similar, the love people have for family. Although they don't celebrate Christmas, my teammates made the holiday special for me. Buying me small gifts and wishing me well. I heart all of those ladies and appreciate all that I learned from them about Chinese culture. I loved our long but entertaining bus rides, funny "I gotcha" sleeping pictures and of course the ladies trying to get me to taste a few Chinese delicacies was interesting. My teammates would have chicken feet in a bag like potato chips. It China this is the norm and my teammates tell me it's pretty tasty. Their sense of humor and competitiveness reminded me of friends back home. We are all so alike. Their pure pride in their country was far from what I expected but I admired their devotion to their country as I am devoted to mine. I loved our conversations on politics, sports and fashion. It got me thinking that maybe if our countries had more women in leadership roles then compromise and a fair resolution may happen faster. But regardless of our differences off the court things seemed to be coming together seamlessly on the court. We were getting ready to go to the playoffs, when I got a call from the WNBA asking me if I wanted to be in the Celebrity All-Star during the NBA All-Star weekend. I thought that was a really cool opportunity and that it'd be a great getaway to hit the reset button before going into the playoffs in China.

The owner of my team, Liang Zhihong, was so gracious to me and they offered to pay for my flight from China back to LA so that I could play in the game and then come back right before we were set to play in the playoffs. So of course I accepted the offer and I took off to LA. It was a great time. I got my hair done once I got to LA (which ladies you know was a must) out there and I had the chance to hangout with my girls. I played in the celebrity game and was on a team with Justin Beiber, Trey Songz, Jalen Rose, Rob Kardashian and our coach was the great Magic Johnson himself. I love everything that Magic Johnson represents as a person, businessman, philanthropist and ambassador for growth in the African American community. He's just an example of the possibilities in this world for so many. Every time Magic sees me he always has a big smile, gives me a hug and asks me how I'm doing. I remember this time distinctly though because it was at the 2011 All Star game in LA. A few years before that Magic was working with TNT and I was in Detroit at the time and I was at one of the Pistons games. I went in the back and was talking to Kenny Smith, Charles Barkley, and Magic, my boyfriend was with me at the time so I brought him back and introduced him and he had a chance to talk to them for a little bit as well. From that time on every time Magic would see me he would ask me how I was doing and how my boyfriend was doing. Not many people take the time to ask you that so it always meant a lot to me when Magic would take the time to do that. He always had a big smile and was very friendly. Well this time he asked me just as he always does and I told him I was single and very happy. He looked at me and gave me a big smile and said: well that's all that matters then. I gave him a big hug and said thank you. It meant a lot to me for some reason. I'm big on signs and it was just another small sign that let me know that my happiness is what matters the most. People think every time athlete's see each other we just talk sports. Well I appreciated Magic's concern to just ask how I was doing instead of just talking sports. I took that with me and I still remember it to this day for what it was worth. Thanks Magic.

It was a great time in LA playing in the celebrity game along side Jalen Rose, Justin Beiber, Trey Songz and Magic Johnson as our coach. I was having a blast out there, just enjoying life and taking a break from the grind in China. I needed that little break and it was so unexpected but a blessing nonetheless. After a fun weekend, I headed back to China and it was time to get down to business for the playoffs.

In China we were playing really well. We were a really young team so no one expected anything from us. We played together as a team and we were really close. This was year two for me and I was excited for our team to take the next step. We made it to the Finals that year and we were so excited to be there because no one thought we would make it that far. It felt good to be there I must say because it was in line with how everything had been going in my life. Maybe I was more focused this time and was able to help my team even more than the previous year when we were put out in the first round. One of my favorite artists, Mary J. Blige sings 'No More Drama' and this is how I was feeling.

In the finals we met up against one of the Military teams from Northern China. One of the best players in China, Miao Lijie, played on this team. In the past Miao had played one season in the WNBA. She was a fierce competitor and beloved by all of China. They were a very strong team, as you'd assume. They were very disciplined players and really executed their game plan well. After tying the series at 2-2 on our home floor the decisive game 5 would be held on their floor. It was a very close game and we were neck and neck the entire game. The game came down to the final seconds. We ended up having to foul in the final seconds and we got another possession. On this possession we ran a diversion play for me. My teammate got the ball and drove it hard to the rim. She pulled up for a short jump and it bounced off. Our big post got the rebound and got hammered on the put back but no foul was called. Yes, my face still twists up when I think about that foolishness. We had our opportunity but the time expired. We'd lost the game in the final seconds on their home court by one point. It was a very tough loss for me. I was so upset that I couldn't close it out for us. I was thinking "should I have demanded the ball and taken the shot myself?" But the reality was we're a team. My teammate that took the shot was hot all game. I had confidence in her and she was cooking the player guarding her all night. So there was no room for would've should've could've thoughts. My heart was hurting for my teammates because I'd won my Championship in the WNBA back home and then won another Championship at the World Championships and hoped that I could've helped them win the WCBA Championship as well. It would've meant so much for them. It would have really helped them gain more visibility and open up lots of new opportunities for them and their families and put them on another level in their Country. Being a champion is something you will have for the rest of your life. People can never take that away from you and as my teammate told me, it helps you make more money. Lol I told her "I know that's right!" That's why I was so upset that we lost. My teammates on the other hand handled it well and were very positive. Their heads were held high and they were happy. They were just so grateful to have even played in a game 5 in the finals. They understood that we were a young team and that we'd made it much farther than anyone thought we would and that was enough for them. Seeing that they weren't too hurt by it, I was able to pick my head up and head on back to the states knowing that we gave it our all. From the coaching staff down to my translator named Nemo, everyone worked extremely hard so I was and still am proud of that team, Jiayou!

Building Blocks

I returned back to the states in February 2011 and I hit the ground running. I was still in my zone and feeling really good about my life. It was my desire to stay focused on building my brand and my business. I wanted to continue putting the pieces of the puzzle together and get on my way to one day being a mogul in my own right. Hey, we all have dreams, right? I went back to Pittsburgh to spend some time with my family and get some things going.

My mom and I decided to start a company in the real estate space called "Cash Building Blocks." The goal of the company would be to purchase low-end homes and then fix them up so that they can be rented or sold to low-income families. This was my way of giving my profit a purpose. It wasn't about money but about doing something good in the community. My mom worked for the McKeesport Housing Authority so she knew all she needed to know about how we would go about this so she was my property manager. We purchased our first home in March and started fixing it up with my Uncle and a few contractors. We were moving in the right direction. I was so excited that my first business was off the ground and there was a lot of room for growth. You never know if something is going to take off or not but it's best to have it and not need it then to need it and not have it.

I was doing a lot of moving and shaking and working on my brand. I did an amazing photo shoot with the great Derek Blanks in Atlanta. I did some magazine spreads and some appearances. It felt really good to be able to be free and focused. It had been awhile since I had been in front of the camera like this and it felt so at home. Some people don't know that I used to model in high school before I got married to the rock – the game of basketball of course! I was able to go as I pleased and I didn't have to check in with anyone or have any negative energy around me. My life was full of positivity and I was enjoying every minute of it.

It's amazing to see how things begin to happen in your life when you let go of unnecessary drama. When you close a door that needs to be closed you allow God to start opening doors that need to be opened. If you just have the faith to let go and let God, He shows up and shows out in your life. I'd taken the blinders and the chains off and I was starting to soar towards my purpose and my goals. The only person that could stop me was me, and I had no intentions of doing that. Life is what you make it and I learned that the hard way. Anywhere you are in life you made an appointment to be there. I started setting new appointments for my life.

Back To Business in the WNBA

It was time to get back to my team and see if we could make another run. My year had been going pretty well minus a couple bumps in the road. We were a good team in the 2011 season but the same feeling wasn't there as it was in 2010. We were just as talented but not as focused and cohesive. There were some injuries that we suffered and that took a toll on our team as a whole. We also lacked the chemistry we needed to string wins together. It was good work that we were putting in but we weren't clicking on all cylinders, as we were the previous season.

Then it was time for our All-Star break and I was blessed to be selected to the team again this season. I was very happy with that and it was something that I always take very seriously. I went to the game and my family was in the stands and it was a good feeling for me. I played hard and showed up on the court again this year. After the game they announced the MVP and it just so happened to be yours truly. I was so surprised because my team lost the game! This had never happened before! Of course, when they called my name my two UCONN girls Tina and Renee had jokes. They had me laughing so hard acting like I stole an election. I leave that to the politicians (or the writers on ABC's Scandal). I had no say in this vote, but I'll take it! When you're in the All-Star game you're literally playing against the best players in the world so it would be very easy for the award to be given to anyone that does well in the game. The fact that I was chosen was another good sign for me. I became the only player in WNBA history other than Lisa Leslie to win two All-Star MVP awards. That's a huge honor in my eyes because the WNBA has the best players in the world.

After the All-Star game it was time to get back to the regular season play. We were still struggling as a team because we were still dealing with injuries and it was very hard to do it without key players. We played to the best of our ability. We were defending champs but we weren't necessarily playing like it. We didn't have what it would take to win the championship again which was tough to swallow, but they always say get to the playoffs and see what happens. You can try your best but as a team you're only as good as your weakest link. You have to be selfless, buy into one another and trust the system. If it wasn't broke, why try and fix it? With injuries and the lack of chemistry it definitely cost us on the court. I played hard and every player that touched the floor played hard and that was all we could ask for. It just wasn't meant for us to win back-to-back championships, which we all had to come to grips with.

There were still steps for me to take, as I was pulling closer to my goal year of 2012. My work wasn't done yet even though my WNBA season was over. My off-season wasn't an off-season for me. The Olympics would be coming up in 2012 and I needed to start getting ready.

Olympic Hopes

The season was over and now it was time for us to begin training for the 2012 Olympic team again. The committee made us aware that there would be a trial in October during the WNBA finals. Everyone that isn't playing in the finals would be expected to be in Italy for the trials. I thought to myself, here we go again this positioning yourself to be picked for the team. I was still feeling it from 2008 when I'd sacrificed so much to make it and didn't. But regardless of what happened in the past this was my shot at it again. This is the goal that I'd set for myself and I wasn't going to let a bad experience keep me from it. I'd already sacrificed up to this point so it didn't make any sense to quit now.

I knew that my teammate Sue wouldn't be able to make it to Italy because she'd had hip surgery. I also knew of someone else who wasn't going to be able to make it because she would have surgery as well, so I was expecting a couple players to be missing. I knew that I was healthy this time around and I didn't want to have any excuses nor any regrets when they made the final selection for the team. I packed my things and I flew over to Italy to be a part of this Euro tour.

Low and behold I arrive in Italy and there are only seven ladies over there. Yes, seven! I was shocked beyond belief. What are we supposed to do with seven players we all joked? There was actually going to only be six players because one person had to leave early. Imagine playing a game with six players. What if someone gets hurt or just can't finish for some reason. It became a running joke with Tina Charles, Asjha Jones, Sophia Young, Cappie Pondexter, Renee Montgomery, Britney Griner, and I. We had Dani Robinson with us for two games, but then she had to leave. Asjha Jones had a knee injury so she wasn't able to actually play in all the games. We were all we got, so no need to look around because more players weren't walking through that door. This trip could have very easily begun to look like a waste of time for everyone involved. Coach Auriemma didn't care how many players were there. He wanted to go anyways. He pushed us and started trying to implement his system, which was tough because the players that played for him were familiar with it, but it takes time to grasp the motion/triangle concept. I could tell sometimes by the look on his face that it was getting to him as well. I could see some frustration because it's very hard to train with only seven players. But it wasn't the players fault that were there, it was the hand we were dealt so we all had to work through it.

We were playing in a Euro Tour so we'd play in Italy, Hungary, Spain and Czech Republic. I wish it could have been as fun as the 2010 World Championships but it was tough, I'm not going to lie. But I appreciated each and every woman that was on that trip. We were fighting our way through it and I noticed that the morale started to get low at times. We lost two games during the tour. That may sound like it's normal or like a low number but we don't lose games on the National stage and if we did lose it was mind blowing. There was no reason that we should ever lose, but we were with this particular line up. There wasn't anything we could do about it. We were playing with six players and trying to get by the best we knew how. We were playing out of position, short, and tired. It was a very interesting experience to say the least. But you can dwell on the negative or you can find that silver lining.

I'd played in China, with huge cultural barriers. I'd also had some pretty tough injuries on the court in the past. I'd been through a lot in my life over the past few years. With those things in the tank I had somewhere to pull from. My attitude was different now and I could behave in a different manner. I looked within and I began to motivate myself in the midst of this trip. I reminded myself that I was the oldest player on the team and that I'd been through much worse things than this. I told myself that it was my job to always remain positive despite the circumstance and situation. It was up to me to keep everyone else positive and help them see it in a different light. I had to be a leader amongst women and some I didn't really know that well. We were all WNBA players with one College kid but we had no chemistry so it made it a bit tougher than usual. I stayed positive and I did my best to try to motivate my teammates along the way. I kept my eye on the prize because I knew what I was over there for. This was a step towards my ultimate goal and I had to take this step and be grateful for the opportunity.

It's in times like these where you find out who you really are. You either get mad with the bad situations or you remain positive in the midst of the trying times. I used it as a lesson; I believe we all did to some extent. They say that adversity doesn't build character it reveals it.

We finished the Euro Tour and headed back to the states. This trip made me appreciate and respect each one of these ladies even more. It's crazy how things can be revealed to you through trying times. I was glad that I'd made it through it and kept my wits about me. I was really proving to myself that I'd grown so much since 2008. I'd become a full-grown woman and I was very proud of it. We can let adversity make us or break us. The choice is yours.

Back in Atlanta I was getting closer to finding a place to live and I'd pretty much made my decision. I wanted to make that decision before I headed back over to China to play my third season with them. There were several letters coming in from overseas teams from all over but I felt a sense of commitment to the Chinese team. I really wanted to try to help them win a championship. They had become like extended family to me. I appreciated the growth that I experienced in China and I wanted to return.

I made my decision on my new home and on the team I was going to play for and I got ready to head over to China to play my third season. Before I left for China I began getting things taken care of for my place in Atlanta. It was great to have Steve, Patrick and Nate come help me move boxes in and started situating my place and making it a home. I was so proud to finally be settling down and calling somewhere home. I love Atlanta and always wanted to live in a city like that. The culture, the locale, the speed, and everything that comes with it, was perfect for me. Atlanta had so much to offer so I made the decision and now Atlanta is home.

Fourth Quarter

Changing Seasons of My Life

I headed back over to China for the third season in a row. I really felt in my heart that this was the best thing for me to do. My Chinese agents Alex Yam and Michael Liu felt that this would be the year for us to win it all. After losing by one point in game five of the finals the year before, this was going to be our year. This time around was so interesting because I'd watched my teammates grow. I remembered thinking about how the younger players were older, more confident and hungry to be Champions. I was playing with young women whose natural talents had developed well, women who would one day be on the Chinese National Team. It was a great feeling to be there with them again. Everyone was so nice to me and it was just like extended family. I had a translator named Jason this time around. Jason had gone to college in California and loved basketball.

I loved how the girls were into music, curious about American fashion, but like me loved the country they were from. Anytime I needed help and Jason wasn't around my teammates would help me. I loved my nicknames for them, our point guard Rabbit aka Moon, always rocking the coolest Ray Bans. Gigi and QQ were two of my favs. Always making me laugh and knowing every Beyonce and Rihanna song. Let's not forget Wei Wei one of the tallest females in China, who spoke the most English and loved Nike shoes. Then there was Apple, Biscuit, Shin and Bear; oh how I grew to really love those ladies! Separated by race, country and culture but united through love, respect and the game of basketball. Yes I wanted a championship this year. It's in my blood. But I wanted it more for them, for my lovely Chinese sisters.

We played as hard as we could the 2011 season but the injury bug finally found our team. We suffered three ACL tears, which was unprecedented in my eyes. That was a really tough blow for a team to withstand. It hurts to have one player go down, but to have three is next to unbearable. We played hard through it and stayed positive but sometimes even a positive spirit can't overcome physical conditions.

I was so proud of my teammates! We had these high expectations at the beginning of the year not only of ourselves but also from coaches, owners and fans. Yet even in defeat they kept giving all they had and to me, that's all anyone could ask. See, you have to understand a lot of my teammates were similar to me growing up. They came from humble beginnings, so through sports they too were able to support and help their families. I know how that feels to have a gift like this amazing talent to play basketball and the more you win the better life you can give your family. So for me helping my teammates achieve our team goals would help their extended family just like it would help mine. My feeling was that we're all in this together! Having that feeling made it easier for me to leave my family and friends for months to return to play with them.

Being in China with my Dongguang family was another great experience that brought meaning and clarity to my life. I was glad that I went. I had some interesting twists happen while in China. It seems like my life always has a twist coming or going. It certainly makes the journey interesting! But the term "smooth sailing" just never seems to apply to me. A year earlier my 17 year old cousin was shot and killed while I was in China, so dealing with that from afar was heart wrenching. One thing I can say is that no matter what turbulence there has been in my life, God has always been by my side, giving me peace and guidance about the situation. My faith has given me strength to cope and press on.

Another Call

While in China I received another one of those life altering phone calls. (Do you see a trend here?) It was on January 1st, 2012. It was my agent on the phone, so I figured it was a "Happy New Year" call. Boy, was I wrong. Instead he broke the news that I had been traded to the Chicago Sky. Really? Wow... We had heard rumors I was being shopped around but I didn't believe they were true since I was told I wasn't going to be traded. My agent asked me how I felt about the Sky. I don't even remember responding. In the back of my mind I didn't know if it was for real. This phone call was like a bomb dropped out of thin air - again. A lot plays through your mind when you are traded but the reality is you need to regroup fast. I was settled in Seattle and after four seasons there I was comfortable with the city, my teammates, the organization and my self-proclaimed storm crazies. Seattle had become "my community," so much so that I had started giving back and making things happen. Hey, I had kids there! (To clarify, they are kids through my charity, Cash for Kids.)

Yes it was a crazy year and we lost in the first round, but that loss had just made me more determined to do my part to help us win in the next season. Unfortunately, I would not be there for the next season.

This move reminded me once again about the business of basketball. It was a business move. It's about personnel; it's not personal and they didn't treat it that way. So I didn't receive a call from the coach, I received a call from my agent. I guess I could just add this to my list of "calls," Cancer, Olympics, and now…the Trade. Of all my calls, this was probably the least expected. But it was a new year and I was headed to a new city.

It was a tough blow but I had to roll with the punches. I'd certainly been through worse by that point! I'd be heading to my third WNBA team and I had no clue what that would be like, because I didn't have any insight into how the team was built.

Unfortunately, the trade was not the most painful thing that happened at the time. I got another call that shook me to my soul. My uncle had passed away. This meant that my family had suffered two deaths in two consecutive years. It's a lot to handle when you come from a close-knit family like ours.

If you add everything up, things could have been pretty bad for me in China that season, but somehow, by the grace of God, I held it together and weathered the storms. Thankfully, during the whole trade time I had one of my best friends visiting me. Having my friend there to support me and talk me through everything was a blessing. I honestly believe that everything that I'd been through up to this point was preparation to get through any test that life put in front of me.

China was definitely eventful the third time around. After dealing with the trade, the death of my uncle and my team losing in the first round it was time to return home. Time to regroup, refocus and prepare for this new journey ahead. Although I may not have asked for this trade, it happened and it was now time to get excited for Chicago and my new Sky High family.

Almost There

I made it back home to Atlanta in February of 2012. I was glad to be back on US soil and I was ready to get to work. This was the Olympic year and the year I'd been waiting for since 2008. Everything that I'd gone through was all to get back to this point. I wanted another shot at the Olympics and I'd put in so much work to get here. Since 2008 I'd been through some heartache, pain, ups, and downs and finally I was drawing closer to the moment I'd dreamed of. I kept getting signs over the years letting me know that I was on the right track. I did everything I could to stay motivated and focused even with all my "calls" I'd achieved more than some could ever imagine – three Championships in the WNBA, a World Championship, and two All-Star MVP's. What more could I ask for? Well, I wanted that trip to London and my second Olympic Gold Medal.

Now that I was back home in Atlanta I began getting ready for the 2012 season and also moving in to my new home. I was working out and feeling good and trying to stay focused on the task at hand. I loved the city of Atlanta and was very glad that I made it my home.

Then one day before I went to work out, I received a call from Bonnie at the WNBA and they told me that the U.S. State Department wanted to know if I'd like to make a trip over to London in April. They were doing a sports envoy to London before the 2012 Olympics, doing basketball clinics and speaking to the youth in several schools. This was right up my alley since I already do a lot of charity work with Cash For Kids. The trip would be to visit some schools and speak to kids about the importance of education and to answer whatever questions they may have. The only thing was that I wasn't officially on the Olympic team so I didn't understand why they were asking me to go. I loved the idea though because I have a huge passion for kids. I want to do anything I can to help them.

The one thing I didn't like about the trip was that I'd made a vow to myself that I wouldn't visit London until I was going over as an Olympian. Naturally this was a vow that I'd have to break because this was about the kids. I had the time and the desire to do it so I decided to accept the offer and make the trip. I knew it was going to be a great experience and I was excited about the opportunity. I wanted to experience British culture and learn about our differences and similarities. That's one thing that always seems to fascinate me. Americans are so privileged and a lot of us take it for granted and don't realize how great it is to have real freedom. We have the freedom to express, the freedom to dream, and the freedom to do. Not many other places have those same freedoms and visiting other places really has helped me realize just how blessed I am to be an American.

By this time, I'd seen so many places and experienced so many things, but I still wanted to add more to my list. London was definitely a place I wanted to experience. My deepest hope was that this wouldn't be my only time getting a call that I'd be going to

London. I tried not to imagine what that pain would be like if I didn't make the team this time.

The Final Call

Before I went to London for the sports envoy I had some business with my charity planned here in the States. My charity, Cash For Kids, has a spring youth basketball league for the kids in my hometown of McKeesport, Pennsylvania. We are very active with my charity and it's always meant the most to me to be able to give back. I don't believe we are given a platform in life to just sit on it. It's my belief that we have a platform so that we can give back to the world. That's what I strive to do as often as I can. The kids in the league were playing their spring games and I was there watching with my mom, parents and our wonderful volunteers. My mom is Commissioner for the leagues so she's always there working the concession stand, deciding coach vs. referee disputes and making sure our kids have a blast.

The games were coming to a close that day and I told my mom that I was getting ready to leave. I needed to go change clothes because I was going to play some pickup games with some of my guy friends.

I left the gym and while I was pulling up to my mom's house when I received a phone call. It was

Renee Brown, the Vice-President of the Women's National Basketball Association. She is also serves on the USAB committee, so I wasn't sure if this was WNBA or USAB business. I was heading to London in two days so naturally I assumed it could have something to do with that trip. She asked me how I was doing and what's going on in my life these days. I told her that I was home in Pittsburgh and had just finished up at the games with the league that Cash for Kids runs. The conversation was going normally so I was wondering what this call was about at this point. Then she tells me that she was calling me to let me know. The US Basketball Committee had come to their decision about the US Women's National Basketball Team. They'd named me to the team! I'd be going to London in August for the Olympic games!

Everything went silent. My throat closed up and tears started streaming down my face. I tried to speak but my voice was cracking. Renee was starting to speak at the same time and it sounded as if her voice was beginning to crack as well. We were both emotional. She congratulated me on the selection and told me she was very proud of me. She said that she'd been watching me, and she knew that I had worked very hard to get back to this point. "You deserve it, Swin."

I was so thankful but I still couldn't really say too much. I remember telling her that I really appreciated it. But it all still seemed like a dream to me, a dream I was watching from somewhere else but not a dream I was a part of. Somehow I found my voice and I thanked her for calling me. I didn't know what else to say or how to say it. I was trying to rush off the phone so that I could scream before I burst. She seemed to sense my desire to hang up though. She stopped me before I got off the phone. "I know you are heading over to London in a couple days but you can't say anything about being on the team. They want to announce it on live television later on." I remember saying, "Renee, are you kidding me? You really want me to hold this in for more than a week?" She said, "Yes, we have to do it this way." Thankfully she said I could tell my mom because she knows how close we are. But otherwise I had to keep quiet. I agreed, even though I knew what she was asking would be one of the hardest things I'd ever done. Harder even then the work I had done to make the team in the first place!

I got off the phone and I immediately drove back to the Crawford Village Recreation Center where my mom and god-mom were still working. I went in to the concession stand where they were and I closed and locked the door behind me. I looked at my mom and when she saw my face she knew I had been crying. She started to panic and was frantically asking me what was wrong with me. I calmed her down and told her it wasn't anything bad. She said, "Girl don't you ever scare me like that again!" and we laughed it off. Then I began to tell them about the news I had. But before I opened my mouth the tears began to stream down my face because I was so filled with joy. When a daughter cries, her mom cries with her. My mom's face began to mirror mine as I told her that I received a call letting me know that I'd been named to the Women's National Basketball Team. They started yelling "YES!" and getting all exited so I was shushing them and telling them in my quiet voice to keep it down because it's a secret. We couldn't hold it in. We hugged, we laughed and we cried together over that news. Had it not taken all that I went through to get to that point then I'm sure that we probably wouldn't have been as excited. But I had gone through the cancer scare, back surgery, heartbreak and professional upheaval to get here. My mom was there through all of it. I had to share this with her.

This feeling is so hard to explain because words can't fully get across the emotions that I felt. My mom is my rock. She is my everything. I had to let them know because they'd been through the fire with me. They'd seen the ups and the downs. They'd been there through the surgeries, and all the pain that I endured. My mom would give me every ounce of her energy and she loved me with every fiber of her being. My love for her grew so strong and it took over me because without her I know that I wouldn't have made it. She sacrificed more than I could imagine, so that I could achieve my dreams. She walked, she ran, and she carried me at times. She was there when no one else was there. She risked her safety for me at times. My mom isn't supposed to drive at night because she can't see very well. One time I called her crying and stressed out during my senior year in college. We were getting ready to play in the regional finals in Milwaukee. She wasn't going to come to the regional finals because she was planning to come to the final four. Well when I called her upset and stressed she got in her car with my two cousins and drove through the night barely seeing so that she could be there for me in a time of need. She risked her life to drive from Pittsburgh to Milwaukee (Literally, my mom is like driving Miss Daisy!) But she wanted me to know that if I could count on anyone it would be her. When I tell you that this moment meant more to me than words can describe, I mean it. I could try to use every word in every dictionary known to man and I wouldn't be able to convey how much my mom and this moment meant to me.

It feels so much sweeter to share in your triumphs with those that were there during your trials. Success isn't really success if there weren't any struggles on the way. Every test that I'd ever had to take was only in preparation for this testimony. At times, my life was a mess but that mess has birthed this message. I set a goal and I decided that no matter what came my way I'd reach that goal. I couldn't count on everyone to stand by me along the way but I had to go anyways. I'm thankful that God saw fit to grant me the desires of my heart and that he allowed my Mother to be there right by my side to see that all of her hard work and sacrifices were not in vain.

It was all worth it. Every drop of sweat, every single tear, every workout, every sacrifice, it was all worth it. I proved it to myself that anything is possible if you work at it. We are built to last; we just have to want to. The things that I thought might break me actually made me. Finally I'd gotten the call and I was on my way back to the Olympics to see if I could win a Gold Medal.

Pre-Olympic Trip to London

I headed over to London for the Sports Envoy with the U.S. State Department, WNBA and NBA cares. It was great to be on the trip with Sam Perkins, a former NBA player with a big heart and love for kids. It was amazing getting to see English culture and learn about the British as a people. This was my first time visiting London and I was glad that I agreed to go.

We spoke at several schools around London and in Birmingham. We also held basketball clinics for the kids. It felt so good being able to give back abroad. I give back in every city that I play in and it was great to be able to give back in London as well. The experience is one that I'll never forget. The questions that I was being asked were questions that really shocked me. Some of the little girls were asking me how could they tell their parents that they want to be an athlete and play basketball. I was blown away because being an athlete is something that most Americans feel is a birthright but in London it wasn't the same way. There are so many different cultures and in some the little girls didn't feel like their families would accept it if they wanted to play a sport. It was very interesting. It's almost hard to give an answer because what would be so easy to do in America may not yield the same results in other countries.

I really believe that I learned as much as the kids did. I was blessed and inspired from this trip. It's mysterious how helping others seems to help you too. Giving reminds me of what life is all about. It's much bigger than me.

The whole time I was in London I was beaming. I'm sure it was partly because of the news I'd received just a few days earlier. I was over there holding it in all week and about to burst. It was very difficult to be over London, while the media and kids kept asking me if I was going to make the 2012 team and I had to try and talk around it without spilling the beans. I obeyed my orders and I held it, but boy was it hard! I finished my service in London and now it was time to head back to my new team in Chicago.

Starting Over

My first year in Chicago was definitely an interesting one. It was another test for me mentally. Everything was new. I had a new coach, teammates, city, and fans; everything was brand new. This time around was so much different than when I got traded to Seattle. The trade to Seattle was my request. This time around I was truly traded out of the city of Seattle and into Chicago so I didn't know what to expect. Then you add in the fact that the Seattle team was a veteran one whereas Chicago was a very young team. It was an emotional roller coaster for me. I didn't want to step on anyone's toes but I'm a natural leader and a vocal leader at that. It was kind of like going into a field of landmines and trying not to step on something that would blow up in your face. I was just trying to find somewhere that I could fit in and be a great asset to the team.

At the end of the day, I just wanted to add to the team in a positive way. Come in everyday working hard and playing to win. I wasn't bringing an ego in nor was I going to shrink and be invisible. It was a tough balancing act but I had to do it.

Back to Seattle

Before the season started, USA basketball had training camp in Seattle. How ironic... We went to Seattle to play against the Chinese National Basketball Team. This was even more irony for me. Here I was, trying to make a new life in a new city and I had to turn around and travel back to my old city with the fans I loved so much and the some of the teammates I had grown so close to in order to play some of my Chinese sisters in competition. God couldn't have developed a bigger test if He tried.

It was a bittersweet feeling when I got off of the plane in Seattle. Aside from senseless rumors about ill will and hurt feelings, this was the first time I would see the "Storm Crazies" since I had been traded. The Storm Crazies are a special breed of Seattle fans that I love with all my heart. Their passion for the game and love for the team is incredible! I'd actually named them the "Storm Crazies" along with my former teammate Ashley Robinson and the name stuck. It was the branding side of me that kicked in and it worked out well. We designed t-shirts with a character I imagined represented the Storm Crazies fan. The t-shirts also benefitted both the Storm foundation and Cash for Kids. The visit was also bittersweet because I had started doing a lot of work in the community and had adopted a group of middle school girls in the "Influence Her" program of the Boys & Girls Club. I had taken them shopping for school clothes with my teammates, taught them about budgeting and what your clothes say about you, and I made sure they were exposed to women who had made a difference. I had given Seattle and its children my time, talent and treasure – Seattle was like your grown child that moves away but you don't love them any less - so coming back was heart felt.

But I was coming in to handle business and then get back to Chicago. So it was awkward, considering my feelings for the Seattle fans. I'm the type of player that is engaging and genuine with my fans wherever I play. But after so many years, Seattle was special. Even still, I made it through and headed back to Chicago to start the season.

The Windy City

The season in Chicago was definitely a windy one; pun intended. It was an up and down season. We would be winning and then we'd start losing. It was back and forth throughout the season and it was hard to find a groove. Injuries didn't help us out either. I was trying to figure out where I fit in on the team. It can be difficult to find a role that fits you on a new team but I appreciated our coaching staff trying to navigate me through it. I wanted to find what I could do best to serve the team and to help us win. I didn't want to mess anything up and I didn't want to be obsolete either. It was very tough for me because if you're not performing at the level you know you're capable of and you're trying to fit in a system that doesn't seem to have much room for you it can definitely shake your confidence. I just really wanted to figure out how I could help.

This is probably pretty common for players on a new team that they had been traded to unexpectedly. I did my best and I fit in where I could. If I could make a play then I made it. I played my part to the best of my ability and I left the rest in God's hands. I'm probably my toughest critic so I wasn't happy about my individual game being up and down because that was the same way our season was going.

The season was a rough one but I made it through. I'd been around long enough to know how to tough it out and remain positive in the process. It's not in me to pout and complain or be a cancer on the team. I speak my mind when needed and I just shut up and play when it's time to play. Every time I touch the court I try to bring passion and intensity. It's the only way I know how to play. My hope was that I'll continue to grow closer with my teammates and find my role on the team and gel like never before. I definitely believed we had a lot of potential and once we all were in sync we would be a force to be reckoned with. I'd embraced Chicago and was having a great time in the windy city. My teammates were all great players and I felt that we would get it together and start racking up the wins. We had a lot of raw talent that will only get better with time.

This was another season of my life and I know that it will play out well. It would be amazing to be able to come together and win a Championship in Chicago. Anything is possible when everyone on a team buys in and we get all the pieces of the puzzle together. I guess we will see what the future holds for us in Chicago.

The Olympic Games – The Finale

This is it!! This is my last go around. I played in 2004, missed 2008 and now I was back in 2012. This is the finale for me. I want to go out on my own terms and not someone else's. I don't want to be pushed out. I want to leave when I feel it's time to go. I put it out there that this would be my last trip on the US National Team and after this I'd start working more on my life after basketball. I loved every minute of this experience, the good and the bad. The commitment is such a demanding one that after this I just knew I wouldn't have the time or energy to do it. I set a goal. I made a plan. I executed my plan. This is what I'd worked for. This is what I'd hoped for.

Before the games I was so excited and really looking forward to it. Three ladies that I played in college with were on the team with me and my college coach was the Head Coach. That, in itself was an amazing feeling.

I played for Coach Auriemma in college at the University of Connecticut so I knew what to expect. He would demand perfection from our drills, and for us to be punctual to everything regardless of how insignificant it might seem. I knew it would be a transition for him but also for us as players. We had some practice time together but not nearly as much as other countries leading up to the Olympics. We needed laser focus if we were going to win a 5th straight Gold Medal for Team USA. As a team we decided to remain positive, hungry and focused on the task at hand. The bottom line for me was that I was going to London and I was excited about it!

We got to London and my PR team had done an amazing job for me. They put a lot of cool things off the court in place and I was loving every minute of it. I was all over the place! When I didn't have team commitments, I had cool appearances, fun times with family and trendy events to attend. It was just a blast. I was having an incredible time with my teammates during the day and at night I got a chance to experience London with family and friends.

I loved my teammates. It's rare you get to play on a team as comical, laidback and borderline crazy as ours. It was fun to see how all the different personalities blended. A lot of our time in London was spent on a bus to practice, to shootaround and then to games. Needless to say, we all had something to say on the bus, sometimes for no other reason then just to ask, "Are we there yet?" Yes, we kept ourselves entertained, whether it was Angel M (Angel McCoughtry) and Money Bags (me) having our delusional rap battles while Seimone and Diana were being our respective managers or Maya singing gospel while using an app as her piano. Then there was Lindsey throwing a punch line into a conversation or Tina's Jamaican accent surfacing every time we brought up Track & Field. Sylvia constantly wore her headphones on her head (though I'm not sure they were always on). Candace was always multitasking like a true Mom. Tamika was constantly snacking (yes, I call her Mikey) and Asjha was constantly asking me for snacks. Then there was Sue who spent her time giving us tutorials on our new Samsung Galaxy phones. This is the stuff that happens when you have idle time on your hands on a bus. When all else fails, we would turn on the music and let the debate of West vs. East coast Biggie vs. Tupac begin!

On the court playing was a different story for me personally. It was a story that I didn't understand at first but it would ultimately be one of my greatest life lessons.

Any player that's ever had a chance to play in the Olympics is a fierce competitor. Trust me, you don't get to this level and not have a competitive spirit. I'm sure Coach Auriemma and any other coach would tell you the same. As the Olympics got underway, we were dominating our opponents. I wasn't playing as much but trust me, I was sitting on the bench staying ready. As a player your number can be called at any time so you stay ready so you don't have to get ready. I remember before a game shooting around with Diana, and she kept telling me "Stay ready you know there's going to come a moment when he has to call your number." I love Dee. She's always worried about her teammates and keeping everyone loose. But what she didn't know was I was ready but I also was at peace and happy for our whole team. I mean after games I started getting text messages from everyone that had a phone with my number in it. "Why aren't you playing more?" "Is something wrong?" "Are you injured?" You name it I heard it for almost two weeks in London. There were so many questions about my playing time and why I wasn't being allowed to play more during these games. The questions would have gotten to a young me. But the more mature, peaceful me wasn't going to question God's plan. I know my friends, family and colleagues just wanted to see me play knowing this was my last Olympics. Their concern weighed on me. But this moment was bigger than a game for me, bigger than how much I played or how much I cheered. A lesson through it all was being learned.

As more people reached out, my friend Tamika Catchings stepped in. Tamika Catchings, Maya Moore, and myself were growing closer on the trip. We would sit and talk about all types of things. Tamika was a very positive influence in London. Tamika always stayed positive and had a great outlook on every situation. I really needed it at this point. I'd been in the Olympics with Tamika in 2004 and now it was 2012 and here we were again. This trip we grew closer than ever before. Through our faith and sisterhood it all really came down to the bigger picture. We'd all come here for one common goal and that was to win Olympic Gold. That's what we want-ed most and it didn't matter how we'd win it as long as we won it. Tamika told me that I meant more to the team than I realized. She told me that I'm a veteran player and that my attitude carries over the whole team. She told me that I was an impact player and that it didn't matter when I'd get in but when I did I'd always be ready and I'd always make a big play. It's easy to grow negative but when you've been through what I've been through, have the friends that I have and the faith I stand on you can't help but want to spread light and be positive. I owe a lot to Tamika for being there for me and riding it out like a true friend. She was there every step of the way and really put things into perspective with me in London. I saw my blessings from a different angle. While many around me may have focused on the time on the floor, my heart was seeking his mercy and grace off the floor. Yes I'm a competitor so you want to play 40 minutes a game. But I'm also a realist and we had one of the greatest teams of all time, in my opinion. Experiencing that moment with these ladies was a blessing. So when Coach Auriemma called "Schwinn" (Yes, he hasn't pronounced my name right since he recruited me to UCONN...) I stepped on the floor ready to go!

I remember feeling like I just wanted to embrace the moment and let all my worries go. All the ladies on our team had different stories and everyone is always lacking something that they might want but we must be thankful for what we do have. God made a promise to me that He'd get me through it and get me to it. He didn't tell me that He'd give me every minute of playing time that I wanted though. He didn't say London would play out like I desired. I shifted my attitude and my outlook on this situation and I started to be thankful that I was there after all I had been through. I was thankful that I'd come that far and overcame so much to achieve that goal. I basked in the moment and appreciated the opportunity. When I got in the game I played as hard as I could. It was worth every minute of it.

We won the Gold and the tears just streamed down my face on the podium. Everything I've worked for, everything I've prayed for, it was all in that moment that I realized once more the awesomeness of God.

I looked back over this humbling journey and realized that the journey I took to get back to the Olympic Gold was actually more precious than the gold medal itself. No amount of money or trophies or medals can be put on the sacrifice and hard work that I put in to get back to that podium. Nothing can replace what I'd been through and all the lessons that I learned along the way. It was all worth it and I'm glad that I weathered the storms and kept going. In life we tend to focus on the end goal, the reward, but when you look in your rear view mirror you realize that the journey brought you the ultimate gold. Trust me, I loved winning my second Olympic Gold Medal. And I'm grateful that I had the support of so many, but especially of Him, to insure my humble journey led me not only to Olympic Gold but also to inner peace. It was that inner peace that wouldn't allow pride, negativity or ego to get in the way of me appreciating my humble journey.

Note From The Author

A lot of times people go through life dealing with difficult circumstances and make the choice to deal with it privately. I was one of those people, until I realized that my story, my humble journey, wasn't only about me. It was an opportunity to share my story, my thoughts, my fall and my climb from 2008-2012.

Humble Journey isn't my whole life story; I like to say it's a glimpse into my life and my truth. Revealing some of lowest points to the highest of highs in my 4-year journey. It was important to me that this book be a symbol of hope, inspiration, redemption and love. Sharing some of my most intimate thoughts on sports, relationships, business and growth was very thera-peutic and hard at the same time. At the end of the day for me as long people can find inspiration, laughs and genuine growth through the pages of Humble Journey this book has accomplished everything my heart desired.

I always say people never remember how you fall, only how you get back up. In 2008 I was in a very low place spiritually, emotionally, and physically. Over the course of 4 years I took time to grow as a woman, daughter, sister and friend. I pray this book inspires you to find growth and change in yourself and in the world. Is the glass half empty or half full? I guess it depends on whom you're asking. Are you a person moving forward, at a stand still or stuck in your past. My hope is that this book will show you how beautiful growth and moving forward is. Live, Love, Laugh and Grow.

- Swin

Special Thanks

I first would like to give all the glory to GOD. Not for what you do Lord but for whom you are. Thank you Lord for walking through this journey with me and carrying me through when I thought I couldn't go on.

Thanks Mommy for always being in my corner and for loving me unconditionally through all my ups and downs. You have always been my rock and I wouldn't be the woman I am today without your love, sacrifice and faith.

Maxi thanks for walking with me through the darkness to find my inner light. You've been one of my closest friends and I love ya for putting up with me lol.

To my fierce, selfless and amazing team, Jakki Nance and Nate Tepp, Thank You - two small words that mean the world from me to you both. I'm only as good as my team and you both have been a true blessing. I appreciate your loyalty, hard work and faith in my vision. Jakki that limo ride is right around the corner. Thanks to your family Fred, Melanie, Ricky and your brother Jeff, for supporting you on this journey with me. Nate the sky isn't the limit, just our view. Your friendship, support and punch lines have kept a lot of foolishness at bay, on more than one occasion.

Big hugs to Gwen and Lew Perkins, thank you for opening your home and hearts to me when I needed a sanctuary.

To one of the craziest strength and conditioning coaches I know Andrea Hudy. You saw something in me as a skinny freshman at UCONN that I didn't know existed. Thanks for pushing me past my limit and into greatness! You are the cream of the crop.

Thanks to my Paps (Bob Gallagher) for being a great mentor since I can remember. Your love and support has been there way before the cameras were and I will always appreciate that. To all my family and friends in McKeesport, I carry the torch of our city with me around the world, proud of who I am and where I am from.

Hugs to Steve, Kevin, Angie, Big Kevin, Dad and Priscilla for your support, love you.

Big hugs and kisses to all the children that participate in Cash For Kids charity. I love each and every one of y'all. Lisa Pelowsky, Reggie Smith, Brenda Sawyer, Uncle Dennis Cash and all the volunteers I appreciate your commitment to the charity and the cause. Without your support and selflessness we wouldn't be able to do the amazing things we do.

Thank You! Nike, USA Basketball, WNBA, NBA, IMG broadcasting and especially Melissa Baron, Youth Places especially Reggie Smith and Lori Schaller, UPMC, Dongguan New Century organization and players, Chicago Sky, Seattle Storm, Bible study crew Tanisha, Camille, Ashley, Marla, Nancy, Jenny, Ruth and the Wednesday Wonders. To my Originals: Lauren, Sue and Lecoe: I heart you ladies. Tamika Catchings my sis through and through. Jovan Goldstein, Ilene Hauser, Sandy Montage, Mike Cound, Tom Cross, Frank Sanchez, Doctor Maroon, Brian Hagen, Jackie McVittie, Dr Peter Littrup, Dr. Jeff Triest, Jemele Hill, Teresa Edwards, Bonnie Thurston, Donyale Martin, Alex Yam and Michael Liu my Chinese agents, Translators Delphee, Jason and Nemo.

Very Special Thanks to Tony Gaskins Jr., whose guidance and support helped insure my first book became a reality.

Thanks also to Jennifer Deutsch, Brian Barney and the rest of the Doner Advertising crew for all you have done for my brand and branding with my website, logo and this great book cover. But a great book cover also requires an amazing photographer, so I have to give a special shout out to Derek Blanks and his glam team, who took both the front and back cover shots for the book and many of the shots on my website too!

Special Thanks: There are so many people from friends, teammates, coaches, doctors, trainers, etc. I would like to thank but the list would just go on and on. Please know I appreciate every single person that I encountered on this journey. Whether it was for a moment, a season or for a lifetime our paths crossing was planned and ordained. You know who you are and so do I. You are appreciated.

Last but not least to all my fans, you have no idea how much I love you all. I never take for granted your support, faith and loyalty! You all have been Team SC through and through. This isn't the end only the beginning. Rock with me! Team #wegrindin

Thanks for your belief and support!

We've all gotten bad news. A job lost, failing health, loss of a loved one. How would you handle a devastating call you never wanted to receive?

Olympian and WNBA star Swin Cash knows what it feels like because she's been there too. She's gotten "the call." Humble Journey: More Precious Than Gold traces her road from the fateful call in 2008, when she failed to make the U.S. Olympic team a second time, to the call in 2012. Join her on this eventful journey through her professional and personal life and discover why the lessons she learned are more precious than the medal she earned.